BOWIESTYLE

● OVERLOOK OMNIBUS

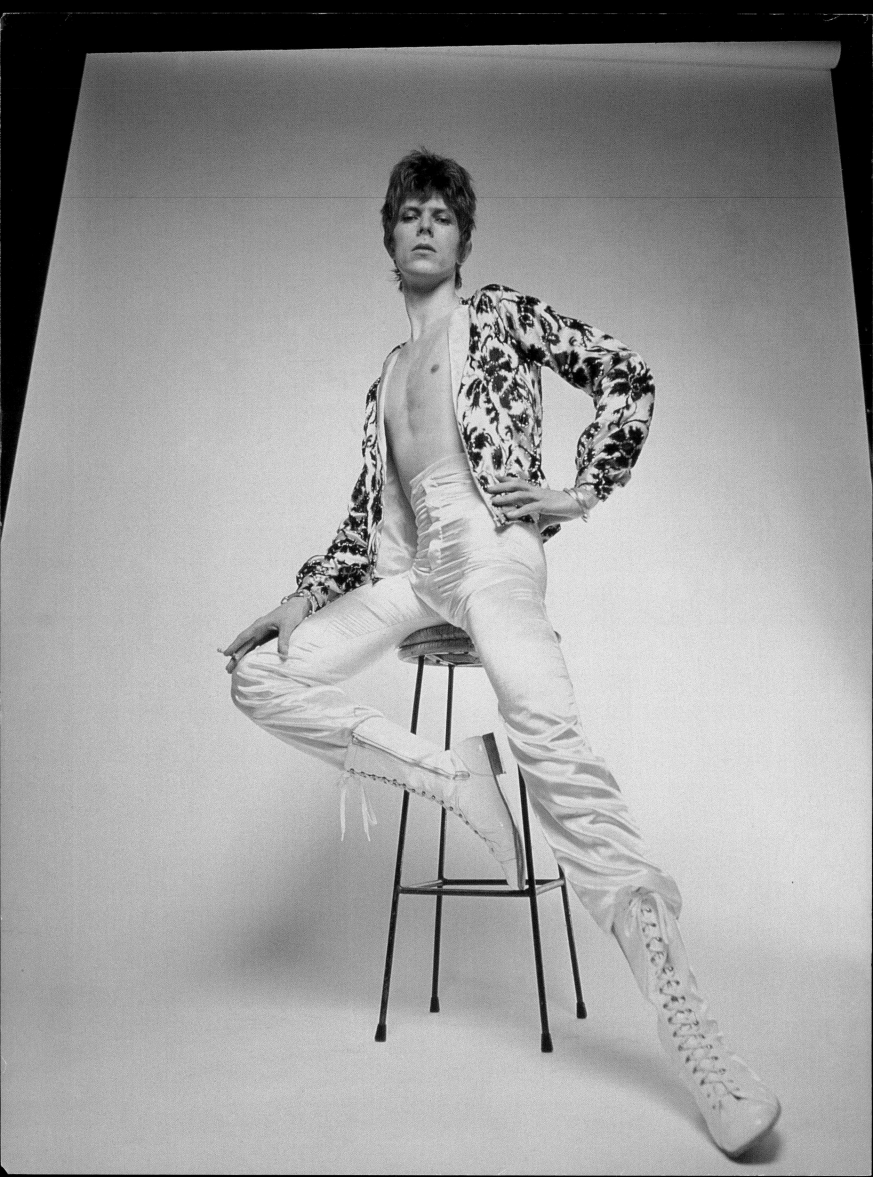

Written by
Mark Paytress

BOWIESTYLE

Including photographs, prints,
paintings and sketches by David
Bowie, Iman, Andy Warhol, Paul
McCartney, Lord Snowdon, Mick
Rock, Terry O' Neill, Andy Kent,
Masayoshi Sukita, Ray Stevenson,
Ken Pitt, Brian Ward, Harry Goodwin
and Steve Pafford.

Designed by
Pearce Marchbank

BOWIESTYLE

Gavin Evans/Retna:Front & back cover,89;Mark Allan:122t; Joel Axelrad/Retna:79b; Brian Aris: 147tr; Clive Arrowsmith/Camera Press:120; Glenn A.Baker/ Redferns: 79r; BBC: 64tl, 147b; Brendan Beirne/Rex: 6; Edward Bell: 128; Paul Bergen/Redferns: 153tl; Peter Brooker/Rex:136t; Larry Busaca/Retna:153c; James Cameron/Redferns:101tc; George Chin/Redferns:152; Corbis: 54b; Fin Costello/Redferns:106b; Courtesy of Crankin' Out Collection: 11,13b,18cl&b,27bl,31c,33,49, 55tr&br,59r,64cl,65,66,67,83tl, 94br,95bl, 112t,118b,142tl, 148lt&b,149, 154tl&r; Bill Davila /Retna: 136l; Debi Doss/Redferns: 16br; EMI:36t,37,139t; Mary Evans Picture Library: 51t&b,100c, 147tc&bl; Chris Floyd/Camera Press:158; Chris Foster/Rex: 43l, 69t; Ron Galella: 55bl; Guglielmo Galvin: 29; Harry Goodwin: 34r,35tr, c&bl,73r, 107cl,118l; Alison Hale/ Crankin' Out: 112b; Dezo Hoffman/ Rex: 4,6,15,19,97t; Dave Hogan/ Rex: 150; Hulton Getty:32t,55tl, 92,108b,114tl,125br,127,133c, 141ct;Mick Hutson/Redferns: 21br; Nils Jorgensen/Rex: 34tc,135; Andy Kent/Retna:9,111l,114c,125c; Jak Kilby/Retna:10,44t; King Collection/Retna:1; John Kirk/ Redferns: 70b; Christian Koller/ Crankin' Out:154c;Jean Pierre Leloir /Redferns: 34b; London Features International:1,3,4,6,7,9,10,12,14t, 16tr,20,21tl,c&c,22t,34tl&c,53tl &br,54l&br,64b,69b,73t,74,75br, 81,82bl,84,85t&bl,c&t&br,91br, 103,106l,107tl&r&cr,108tl,109, 110,111c&b,119,125tr&bl,129, 131b,132b,134,137,139b,140cr, 141bc,142bl&r,143,144,145, 146,151,154b,159bl; Doug McKenzie: 26,27br,36tl; MEN Syndication: 21tr; Pearce Marchbank:100/101b; Robert Matheu/Retna: 148t; Mirror Syndication Int: 57,108cl; Keith Morris/Redferns:79t;

© MTV Europe: 140bl; G.Neri/ Sygma:126tl; Michael Ochs Archive/Redferns:80t,106cl,156; Frank W.Ockenfels III: 54c; Alex Oliveira/Rex: 51c; Terry O'Neill: 98t&bl,102,146t; Denis O'Regan/ Idols: 55t; Scarlet Page/Retna: 48b,130; PA News:159tr; Courtesy of Penguin Books: 146r; Kenneth Pitt: 5,44br,45,48l,52; Pictorial Press:1,3,9,14b,36cr&b,40,42b, 43r,46tc&r,47,48tr,53cr,54t,56t, 60,61bl,80r,82tc, 83bc&r,87tl, 88tr,99,104tr,114tr,115,133r,14 0bc,141br; Photofest/Retna: 6, 114bl; Barry Plummer: 46br,87b, 117b; Pat Pope/Rex:155; Neal Preston/Retna:139c,140c,148r; Michael Putland/Retna:6,73l;RCA: 118r,121l,126b; David Redfern: 23; Redferns: 35tl,105; Lorne Resnick/Retna: 9; Retna:108tr, 141r; Rex Features: 9,10,22b,27t, 28bl,42l,50rt&b,55b,76,82tl,83t r,83bl,85t&bc,86,88br,96,97bl, 100tr,104b&l,107bl,116,117t, 121cr,131t,136bl,138,141c,146cl, 160; Ebet Roberts/Redferns: 78b; Copyright © Mick Rock;1,16tl&c, 38,39,42t&r, 68,71,72,73b,75l, 77,78tl,87tr,90,93,94t,95t,113, 132t,133tl&b,140cl,141t; Photograph by Ethan A.Russell copyright © 1972-2000: 106tr; Nina Schultz: 122b; Corinne Schwab:136br; Wendy Smedley/ Crankin' Out: 112c; Steve Smith/ Crankin' Out:153br; Snowdon/ Camera Press: 123,124; Bob Solly Collection: 32b; Ray Stevenson/ Retna:10,41,44bl,46bl&c,53cl, tc,tr&bl,59b,61b,82bl; Masayoshi Sukita: 17,91bl,112bl,148c; Charles Sykes/Rex: 8; Artur Vogdt: 101c; Wall/MPA/Retna:157; Chris Walter: 91t; Brian Ward: 2,63,70t, 75t; Barry Wentzel:140br; Kevin Wisniewski/Rex:159c; Richard Young/Rex:31cb,94bl,95br,139br, 142tr,159br.

Omnibus Press wishes to thank Steve Pafford for his many vital contributions. He edits Crankin' Out, the irregular but excellent international David Bowie fan club magazine, personally endorsed by David in 1994. Contact Steve, enclosing a SAE/IRC at Crankin' Out, PO Box 3268, London NW6 4NH Telephone 0906-8299 832 (calls cost a maximum 60p/min).

Visit Omnibus Press at www.omnibuspress.com

This edition published by Omnibus Press and distributed in the United States and Canada by The Overlook Press, Peter Mayer Publishers Inc, 141 Wooster Street, New York, NY 10012. For bulk and special sales requests, please contact sales@overlookny.com or write to us at the above address.

Copyright © 2016 Omnibus Press (A Division of Music Sales Limited) 14/15 Berners Street, London, W1T 3LJ, UK.

ISBN 978-1-4683-1389-5

Every effort has been made to trace the copyright holders of the photographs in this book but one or two were unreachable. We would be grateful if the photographers concerned would contact us.

A catalogue record for this book is available from the British Library.

Cataloguing-in-Publication data is available from the Library of Congress.

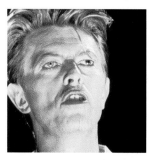

At manager Ken Pitt's flat, London, 1967. Bowie remembers: "At this time I was wondering whether I wanted to be a serious mime or whether I should carry on with music. That's an incredible top." Pitt: "It was an Arabic bolero from Palestine, and belonged to my mother."

Amsterdam, 1977. "I think I have a certain vocabulary that, however much I change stylistically, there is a real core of imagery. I don't see any abrupt changes in what I've done."

An impeccably groomed Mod and a Millennium Man technophile. A riot of sexual confusion and a tanned, uncomplicated symbol of Eighties wealth.

For four decades, David Bowie has been rock music's most conspicuous mannequin and creator of fabulous fads and fashions – and outlived them all.

Bowie's formative years were spent chasing trends, often adding idiosyncratic touches to elevate himself above the crowd. Hitting a creative peak between 1972 and 1976, he transcended street style by reinventing himself into a one-man spectacular, a cultural whirlwind whose series of alter-egos – Ziggy Stardust, Aladdin Sane, the Thin White Duke – were lapped up by his flamboyant and dedicated flock with unflinching devotion.

To his critics, who saw only costume-changes and grand theatrical gestures, Bowie was a clothes-horse who'd fast-tracked to stardom on a tide of hype.

The sneers came thick and fast: Mock Rock, Glitter Rock, Shock Rock, Camp Rock, even Fag Rock, each invoked with a resigned shake of the head. Bowie was an arriviste, an invented star with the airs and whims of a pampered mistress in the hat department at Harrods.

David Bowie revolutionised how rock looked. But he also changed how we looked at stars, and how we listened to music. Prior to his spectacular arrival in 1972, rock aspired to impress musicologists and literary types. Bowie's most enduring influence was to drag rock music back to where the fiercest debates centred on authorship, sexual identity and the blurring of high and low art, debates that were later united under the postmodern banner. Far from smothering rock with foundation cream and elaborate stage sets, Bowie liberated the form, prompting a whole new set of debates and extending its limits.

Yes, Bowie's project was about style and presentation, egos and whims. But beneath the shiny exteriors, those seemingly empty gestures, that lust to be looked at, was a brilliant new rock aesthetic – with David Bowie as its ideologue and showpiece. His playful mix-and-match style wasn't applied only to the costumes.

Irreverence and pastiche also informed his music. He'd take the simple flash of Fifties rock'n'roll, the artful primitivism of little-known American warp-merchants The Velvet Underground and Iggy Pop, and give them a singer-songwriterly sheen. His concept of 'The Star', which he'd discuss with Warholian ingenuity, came gift-wrapped in fiction and artifice.

Bowie's "style" has always amounted to more than clothes, hair and cosmetics. Style, for Bowie, is inextricable from art. It is the books he reads, the paintings he buys, the films he watches. It's also bound up in the way he sees himself and how he lives his life. It is less a flight from reality than an entire way of life; that's what makes him so fascinating. Anyone can adopt a series of guises in the name of art and build a stadium career out of it. In fact, many do. But ultimately, Bowie is less about trappings and more about confronting the traps that seek to limit human potential. That quest has taken him from Beckenham to Babylon, from playful melodramas to the brink of insanity and death.

The point of this book is not to repeat the details of Bowie's musical career, which have been documented many times (though rarely with the thoroughness and insight of Peter and Leni Gillman's *Alias David Bowie*, published in 1986), but to explore his various stylistic guises in the context of their musical and cultural backdrops.

BowieStyle provides the signposts to every transformation, looks at the influences and the icons that helped shape them, and the debates and the controversies that each inevitably provoked.

Only One Paper Left. New York, 1997, wearing Paul Smith: "I like to dress well, but it's not something on which I felt my reputation should be built," says Bowie.

BOWIESTYLE

BOWIE STYLE

Facing page: As the
vampirish 18th century
aristocrat, John Blaylock, in
The Hunger, Luton, 1982.

David Jones at 18 months, at his parents' home in Brixton.

David Bowie's earliest ventures into style conform closely to a textbook reading of post-war subcultural fashions. As David Jones, he developed a youthful passion for rock'n'roll, matured into jazz, then saw a role for himself in the burgeoning rhythm and blues movement. He grew his hair, blossomed into a Mod peacock then, having rechristened himself David Bowie, adopted the pose of a sophisticated Europhile. Unfortunately, there was little demand for such a creature in 1967, when hippie fashions dominated. Hopelessly wrongfooted, David licked his wounds for several months before coming on as Bob Dylan-style folkie, albeit prettier and with an eye for a gimmick. That was the David Bowie the world first glimpsed in 1969 when 'Space Oddity', a faintly macabre interpretation of space travel, gave him his first taste of success.

1.1

The Buddha Of Suburbia

Suburbia spawned the British Rhythm & Blues boom. Punk rock's greatest outrages were created there. And so, too, was David Bowie. Suburbia, a social space favoured by those ostriches of humankind who demanded a peaceful haven away from the grit and grime of urban life, is much-maligned. But its simple ways and suffocating properness have proved time and again to be a valuable creative aid. Nothing arouses imaginations more, it seems, than the comfort zone marked out by net curtains and leafy cul-de-sacs.

David Bowie was often profoundly embarrassed by his years spent in the comfort zone; it just wasn't his style. Biographies usually describe him as "the boy from Brixton", an altogether different social setting and one that suggests excitement, danger and streetwise urban glamour. Not that the young David Jones ever saw much of that: his family had quit south London by the time he was six, opting for a two-up, two-down in Bromley, Kent. That's where David grew up before the allure of central London drew him away.

Years later, in 1993, Bowie recalled the mental landscapes of his youth with a cool, but hardly affectionate score for *The Buddha Of*

Facing page: As early as 1962, Bowie was behaving pseudonymously, styling himself Dave Jay during his year with supper-club combo The Kon-rads. The name was inspired by Peter Jay and The Jaywalkers, who, according to Bowie, were only one of two British bands "that knew anything about saxophones."

St. Matthews Drive, Bromley, scene of Bowie's *Buddha Of Suburbia* video shoot. He gave the shrubbery on the right a damned good kicking.

SHAPING UP

Suburbia, a four-part television adaptation of Hanif Kureishi's 1990 novel. The project was tailor-made for him. Kureishi was a Bowie enthusiast who'd also plotted his escape while attending Bromley Tech; Bowie could hardly have failed to recognise himself in the title, even if the book's pop-seeker was based on a comtemporary of Kureishi's, punk star Billy Idol.

It could be said that David's first infant outfit, a nappy, later influenced the Sumo wrestler's truss he wore on stage in 1973, but the building-blocks that helped shape his life, and the way he presented himself, had little to do with clothes. A likeable schoolboy and a popular Cub, with a keener interest than most for playing Cowboys and Indians, David was introduced to life beyond the comfort zone by his half-brother Terry. Terry, who was several years older, was a jazz enthusiast with Beatnik ways. Often absent, his influence was primarily symbolic: he became David's first idol whose wayward ways inevitably nourished his sibling's later nonconformity.

An outsider by virtue of his status as Peggy Jones' son from a previous relationship, Terry continued to exercise a strange hold on David's imagination until his suicide in 1985. After he fell ill during the mid-Sixties and was diagnosed with schizophrenia, an illness that seemed to run in the family, Bowie was frightened yet fascinated. From the split personas of the Seventies to individual songs (one, 'All The Madmen', famously proclaimed that asylum inmates were "all as sane as me"), insanity became an enduring theme in Bowie's work.

David Jones' fantasy life was further fuelled by America, a Technicolor funhouse stuffed with gadgets and dream-factories, and rock'n'roll, which introduced a strange-looking, and even stranger-sounding, cast of miscreants into his life. He was nine in 1956, when rock'n'roll swept through Britain, but already old enough to plump for two of its most visually striking stars – mean'n'moody Elvis Presley and flamboyant Little Richard. Stars fascinated David. His father gave him an autograph book and took him backstage to meet Tommy Steele. David became hooked on fame.

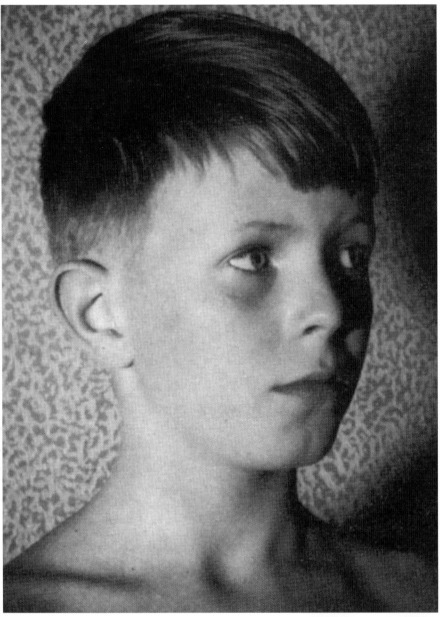

The boy David. By 1953 the Jones family had swapped Brixton for Bromley - "the crummy bit," Bowie recalled.

Aladdin nappies in Glasgow, 1973.

Facing page: May 1964. Tonight, Matthew, I'm going to be Tommy Steele.

Bowie: "I was always accused of being cold and unfeeling. It was because I was intimidated about touching people."

"Sometimes I don't feel like a person at all, I'm just a collection of other people's ideas." You wouldn't have heard Mick Jagger, Bob Dylan, or Pete Townshend talking like that, but in June 1972, as Ziggymania was transforming him into the most discussed performer in pop, David Bowie was turning the concept of The Star on its head. It seemed as much about manufacture and manipulation as it was music.

As the year began, Bowie had playfully predicted his own stardom, and then let his alter-ego, Ziggy Stardust, do all the hard work for him.

The media gleefully dubbed him "The first rock star of the Seventies" knowing full well that the phrase had been concocted by Bowie's manager. For 18 months, Bowie/Ziggy played the part of the Superstar to the hilt. Only favoured journalists and photo-graphers were given access to him; tours of Britain, America and Japan were conducted in a manner usually reserved for royalty; a phalanx of burly bodyguards surrounded Bowie at all times, while the attendant entourage travelled every-where in limos. A mantra, "Mr. Bowie does not like to be touched," was recited as if safe passage to a blissful afterlife depended on it. In

emphasising the manu-facture of stardom – using fictitious aliases, hype, and revelling in Hollywood-like plasticity – Bowie both uncovered and exploited the pop fantasy. The art was in the deconstruction; the out-come, as Bowie had always intended, was the real thing. What he couldn't have predicted was the scale of his success; how, like the legends of Garbo or Valentino, the more remote and 'false' he became, the more his popularity grew. No one had reckoned with the repressed desire for old-style stars – glamorous, larger-than-life and endowed with unfathomable mystery.

David Bowie wasn't the first manufactured Superstar, but he was the first to make the 'creation' an integral part of his enter-prise. By using the device of an alter-ego, Ziggy Stardust, his bid for fame was both a quest and a goal. It is this distancing technique that lies at the heart of Bowie's achievement. Pre-Ziggy rock artists (with the possible exception of Bob Dylan) were essentially one-dimensional men whose talents were measured according to the rules of poetic or musical competence. Bowie widened the rules to include visual elements, then bent them completely out of shape with a 'knowingness and nothing-ness' clause that dragged artifice into art. It was the end of innocence.

Lest we make the same mistakes as our less enlightened predecessors, the Bowie effect also im-pacted on musical style. The seeds of a potential crisis had already been sown by Marc Bolan, whose tinsel

take on Fifties rock'n'roll had enraged progressive purists who suspected it was merely nostalgia via the back-door. As *Melody Maker*'s Roy Hollingworth commented in April 1972: "Is it your turn to tell the younger generation that they don't know what real music is?" he asked readers.

Bolan's revival of the three-minute, three-chord song form indeed flouted rock's two-decade advance. But was it so bad? Hadn't the rush to become a respectable art form based on the archetypes of literature and classical music prompted a seepage of double-LPs where preposterous morality plays, often inspired by Tolkien, would be played out to the sound of frenzied muso sparring.

Against this background, Bowie's fleet-footed contrivance of an alternative rock canon – which included American sleazoid trashmongers Iggy Pop and The Velvet Underground,

"The jacket was a French import made of nylon, though it had a leather look. He called this outfit his 'James Dean plastic look' and posed with that attitude: Ziggy Stardust, movie star, sighted in Hollywood, exposed for your pleasure." - photographer Mick Rock.

and Midlands miscreants Mott The Hoople – inevitably offended critical sensibil-ities. Like Bowie's ersatz star pose, the effects weren't really felt until punk.

When Bowie made his grand entrée in 1972 with Ziggy Stardust, he played a cat-and-mouse game with one of rock's central referents – identity.

As Ziggy became Aladdin Sane, and Bowie a "grasshopper" for whom role-play was a more gainful pursuit than the spurious notion of 'finding himself', the very foundations of rock shuddered. Bowie declared he was gay, played the part of an androgyne from alien parts and forced audiences to confront their sexuality. The certainties came tumbling down. His concerts became multi-media extravaganzas incorporating mime, theatre and film. His songs, deceptively simple but skilfully administered, may even have been pastiches. David Bowie could be artfully highbrow or shamefully crass, a Romantic visionary or a postmodern bricoleur before such a thing was ever contemplated. One thing was definite: during 1972 and 1973 he altered the look, the sound and the meaning of rock'n'roll. For this achieve-ment alone, he secured a vital place in history.

Above: The "singing boutique" in action.
Left: Greta Garbo and Rudolph Valentino, detached idols from cinema's silent age.

Facing page: Bowie dressed in a quilted black plastic body suit, designed by Kansai Yamamoto, who commented: "Bowie has an unusual face. He's neither a man nor a woman. There this aura of fantasy that surrounds him. He has flair."

David's father Haywood Stenton 'John' Jones, worked for children's charity Dr. Barnado's Homes. Bowie would occasionally sing for the orphans in the Sixties.

John Jones was a firm, conventional man whose chief influence on his son was his lower middle class reserve. Years later, Bowie recalled his father's "iron discipline" and the wartime mentality that scarred his parents' generation. In a 1968 interview in *The Times*, he complained: "We feel our parents' generation has lost control, given up, they're scared of the future... I feel it's basically their fault that things are so bad." The innocence and happiness of childhood is something Bowie revisited several times during his early adult life. There was nothing ambivalent about a line like "I wish I was a child again / I wish I felt secure again", which he sang in 1966. His first LP, released the following year, was virtually a lament to a vanquished childhood: "There Is A Happy Land," he insisted, where "adults aren't allowed".

Puberty broke the spell of universal brotherhood and encouraged competition and, in turn, personal development. At Bromley Technical High School (1958-63), the teenage David liked art and chased girls. More than that, the lanky schoolboy developed a compulsive need to stand out from the crowd, and test the bounds of popular taste. These two school photographs reveal the transformation. On the left, in 1959, the pre-teen David, with his regulation haircut and smart uniform, looks every inch the model pupil. For the second (*below*), taken in 1962, his body is angled provocatively, his head crowned by a bizarre, space-age quiff, a thick blond streak added for dramatic effect. He'd become the classic teenage rebel, all attitude and self-consciousness.

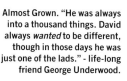

Almost Grown. "He was always into a thousand things. David always *wanted* to be different, though in those days he was just one of the lads." - life-long friend George Underwood.

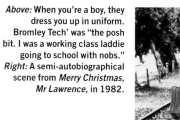

Above: When you're a boy, they dress you up in uniform. Bromley Tech' was "the posh bit. I was a working class laddie going to school with nobs."
Right: A semi-autobiographical scene from *Merry Christmas, Mr Lawrence*, in 1982.

Facing page: "I didn't mind a sense of elegance and style as a child, but I liked it when things were a bit off. A bit sort of fish-and-chips shop."

Facing page: Bowie celebrated his 50th birthday with an all-star bash at Madison Square Garden, New York, 1997.

On 9 January 1997, Bowie celebrated his 50th birthday (a day late) in front of a 20,000-strong audience at New York's Madison Square Garden. There was no Spiders From Mars revival. No Iggy Pop or Mick Jagger or Tina Turner. Instead, Bowie surrounded himself with some of his sharper friends, like Sonic Youth, The Smashing Pumpkins' Billy Corgan, Foo Fighters, ex-Pixie Frank Black and The Cure's Robert "What do I do with this lipstick?" Smith. The only other old boy was Lou Reed. Sometimes, though, it suits the young pretenders to seek Bowie out…

Suede
Twenty years later, the "I'm Gay… but then again maybe I'm not" strategy was revived by Suede's Brett Anderson. It won Suede a few extra magazine covers, and secured the insatiable Anderson an audience with Bowie for an *NME* 'summit meeting' and cover.

Nine Inch Nails
Trent Reznor's pretty hateful noise machine hitched a ride on the US leg of Bowie's *Outside* tour which, by no coincidence, featured the NIN-influenced 'Hallo Spaceboy'. Reznor has remixed a couple of Bowie songs, 'The Hearts Filthy Lesson' and 'I'm Afraid Of Americans', and has taken to working with several of Bowie's backing musicians.

Morrissey
Glam aficionado Morrissey shared a stage with Bowie in 1991 for a version of Marc Bolan's 'Cosmic Dancer', and coaxed Mick Ronson back to produce his 1992 album, *Your Arsenal*, which included the Bowie-esque 'I Know It's Gonna Happen Someday', complete with 'Rock'n'Roll Suicide'-style coda. "David Bowie doing Morrissey doing David Bowie" was too good to miss, said Bowie, who promptly re-recorded the track for *Black Tie White Noise*.

Nirvana
David Bowie's reputation received an unexpected boost when Kurt Cobain's group of grunge stalwarts gave a sterling performance of 'The Man Who Sold The World' for an MTV *Unplugged* TV special in 1993.

Just a few months later, Cobain had, in his mother's words, joined "that stupid club", a real-life "rock'n'roll suicide". Five years, that's all he got.

Placebo
Panda-eyed Brian Molko has studied Bowie's strategies closely. And he's been generously rewarded with a studio collaboration, 'Without You I'm Nothing', plenty of namechecks, and a joint appearance with David Bowie on the 1999 Brit Awards show.

A rare publicity shot of
The Kon-rads, circa 1963.
"We wore gold corduroy
jackets, I remember, and
brown mohair trousers and
green, brown and white ties,
I think, and white shirts.
Strange colouration."

The dilated pupil in Bowie's
left eye, the apparent legacy
of a punch-up with pal
George Underwood, may,
some suggest, have actually
been caused by an accident
with a toy propeller.

By 1962, the Teddy Boy look already belonged to
the previous decade, but stray remnants of the
style – narrow tie, drainpipe trousers – could still
earn reputations for 15-year-old boys. Already,
styles were being mixed, and David's winklepicker
shoes and button-down shirts, both recent imports
from Italy, were evidence of the emerging
Modernist look, a sophisticated, aspirational style
that contrasted with the Teds' aggressive working-
class stance. Bowie later enthused about the new
breed to journalist Timothy White: "These weren't
the anorak Mods (who) turned up on scooters…
They wore very expensive suits; very, very dapper.
And make-up was an important part of it; lipstick,
blush, eyeshadow, and out-and-out pancake
powder… It was very dandified."

Chic, modern and highly individualistic, the
Mod ethic proved instantly seductive to aspiring
peacocks like David Jones and his mate,
George Underwood. But their competitiveness
sometimes strayed beyond fashion and music.
An argument over a girl called Deirdre in 1962
ended when George walloped David in the eye,
leaving him with an indelible characteristic that
even surpassed his left-handedness for marking
him out as 'different' – a permanently dilated pupil
in his left eye that leaves the impression that one
eye is much darker than the other.

The King Bees, 1964.
George Underwood is on
the far left. David claimed
the other members were
"some guys from Brixton I
met in a barber's shop"

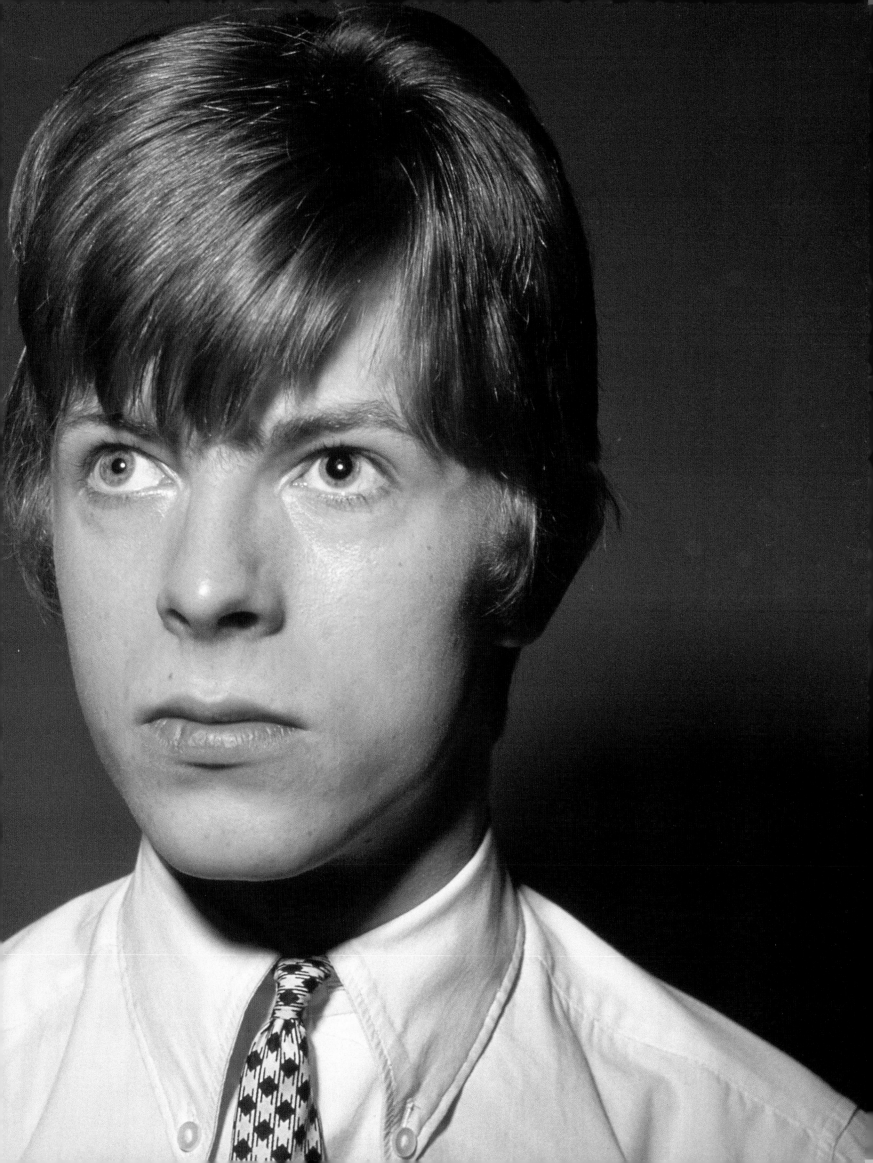

Influences and heroes play an enormous part in Bowie's life and work.

A born enthusiast, who can't help but share his passion for little-known writers or new musical fads, Bowie virtually invented off-the-peg cultural capital single-handedly. Commodity fetishism? Perhaps. An empty display? Well, he does have a fast turnover rate, but that's more likely a reflection of his thirst for new ideas.

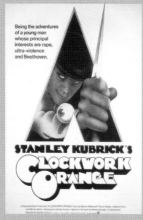

A Clockwork Orange
Stanley Kubrick's film of Anthony Burgess's novel proved so disturbing that the director withdrew it from cinemas just a year after its release in 1971. Promoted as "the adventures of a young man whose principal interests are rape, ultra-violence and Beethoven", the movie was plagiarised by Bowie for its look, its 'nadsat' (street slang), and its theme music, Wendy Carlos's Moog take on Beethoven's 'Ode To Joy', which was used to herald the Spiders' arrival on stage during 1972 and '73. The piece reappeared as intro music for Bowie's 1990 Sound + Vision tour.

Films and film idols have provided Bowie with an endless source of material. He's nicked a few titles for his songs, a few images for his album covers. He's even made one or two memorable contributions to the silver screen himself.

Un Chien Andalou
Dead donkeys rest inside pianos. A woman, dressed in masculine-style attire, pokes at a severed hand. A cyclist inexplicably falls off his bike. Anonymous breasts are fondled. But before all this, a woman's eye is opened and neatly slit with a razor. The film is *Un Chien Andalou*, a masterpiece of avant-garde cinema concocted by surrealist mischief-makers Salvador Dali and Luis Bunuel. Apart from the time Roxy Music supported him at the Rainbow, this 17-minute short – projected before his 1976 Station To Station shows – is the best support act Bowie's ever had. And, perhaps, the inspiration for that memorable "throwing darts in lovers' eyes" quip.

Metropolis
Fritz Lang's 1926 masterpiece of German Expressionist cinema, a futuristic study in glorious art deco, was brought to Bowie's attention by Amanda Lear. After viewing the film, early in 1974, he devoured everything he could find on Lang and related subjects. Several years later, Bowie was poised to bid for the film rights, until producer Giorgio Moroder beat him to it. *Metropolis*, and another Expressionist classic, *The Cabinet Of Doctor Caligari*, provided the inspiration for the stark imagery of the 1976 stage shows.

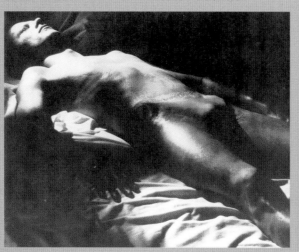

Bowie playing the alien in Nic Roeg's 1976 film, *The Man Who Fell To Earth*.

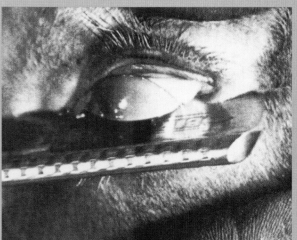

Bunuel and Dali's surrealist short, *Un Chien Andalou*, with its controversial eye slitting shot, provided a shocking support act for Bowie's 1976 tour.

INFLUENCES AND HEROES

Richard Burton plays 'Angry Young Man' Jimmy Porter in the 1959 movie, *Look Back In Anger*. Mary Ure, left, and Claire Bloom, right, co-star.

'Wild Is The Wind'

Bowie revived the title song of this 1957 George Cukor melodrama, starring Anna Magnani and Anthony Quinn, for *Station To Station*. However, he probably came to it via Nina Simone's Sixties recording of the song, which he has cited as his favourite ever recording.

'Starman'

That chorus sound familiar? "It was actually meant to be a male version of 'Over The Rainbow', " confessed the man once described as a "Judy Garland for the rock generation". The song was made popular by Garland in the 1939 evergreen, *The Wizard Of Oz (below)*.

'Beauty And The Beast'

Jean Cocteau's magical interpretation of the fairy story was filmed in 1945 as *La Belle Et La Bete (below)*. Bowie recorded his version for 1977's "*Heroes*".

'Look Back In Anger'

This John Osborne play, a key Angry Young Man text, was filmed by Tony Richardson in 1959 and popularised the idea of the solitary male raging against his sorry lot.

Lodger

Roman Polanski's 1976 movie, *The Tenant*, was a morbid study in paranoia and insanity, and a likely, though rarely acknowledged, source for the *Lodger* album title.

'Dead Man Walking'

Sean Penn directed and co-starred with Susan Sarandon in this Oscar-winning true story from the mid-Nineties.

'Seven Years In Tibet'

Heinrich Harrer's account of an ex-Nazi on the run from the Allies, who journeys to the mountains of Tibet where he befriends the Dalai Lama, provided an ideal launching-pad for a Bowie song.

2001: A Space Odyssey

Stanley Kubrick transformed an Arthur C Clarke story into a mesmerising cinematic acid trip in 1968. The denouement – a spaceman drifts into oblivion – was a clear inspiration for Bowie's 'Space Oddity', which also owed some of its success to the space race that ended on July 20, 1969 when Neil Armstrong became the first man on the moon.

1.2

It's A Mod, Mod World

Between 1963 and 1966, London became the style capital of the world. Galvanised by the resounding thud of the Beatles-inspired beat boom, Britain's first post-war generation cast off the National Service mindset in favour of a riot of self-expression. Carnaby Street was awash with boutiques, scooters roared down busy city streets and the state of the nation debate centred on the length of young men's hair.

David Jones, already on intimate terms with his bedroom mirror, was perfectly poised to join the cultural revolution. He was obsessed by stardom, taste and style which, in true Mod fashion, would change with the weather. His attention to such matters gave him his first taste of media controversy when, in November 1964, he was invited onto a television show to defend the right of young men to grow their hair. His first concern, though, was carving a niche for himself on the music scene. Unfortunately, it was the era for groups, so David was forced to throw in his lot with other musicians. It was a frustrating period for him, with success proving more elusive than he might have imagined.

A newly peroxided Davie Jones with The King Bees performing 'Liza Jane' on BBC2's *The Beat Room*, June 1964.

Portrait of a young man as an art buff. In satin trousers at manager Ralph Horton's flat in 1966.

"I didn't like riding scooters," admitted Bowie. Though that didn't stop him having this one customised for promotional purposes years after the Mod boom.

Wearing Chelsea boots and three-button suit with double back vent: "I didn't really like the Teddy clothes too much. I liked Italian stuff. I liked the box jackets and the mohair. You could get some of that locally in Bromley, but not very good. You'd have to go right up to Shepherd's Bush or the East End."

PAINTER MAN

I Am A World Champion, 1977, (*below*). "In neither music nor art, have I a real style, craft or technique. I just plummet through, on either a wave of euphoria or mind-splintering dejection."

With 1976's *Head Of J.O*, his portrait of Iggy Pop, Los Angeles, 1990 (*below*). In the early Nineties, Bowie renamed his song publishing company Tintoretto Music, after the Italian Renaissance painter.

Paul McCartney's *Bowie Spewing*, 1990 (*right*). David: "When you are an artist you can turn your hand to anything, in any style. Once you have the tools then all the artforms are the same in the end."

During the early Seventies, David Bowie transformed rock by applying contemporary art concepts to a medium that lived in the shadow of 19th century Romanticism. He compared himself to a Rosetti painting, name-dropped Andy Warhol to anyone who'd listen, and sought to elevate rock performance to the status of high art. Bowie even patronised Belgian artist Guy Peelaert, who was commissioned to paint the cover of the 1974 LP, *Diamond Dogs*.

Bowie was an aesthete, for sure, but a practising fine artist? Not according to this quip made during a 1973 interview: "When I was an art student I used to paint but when I decided I was no good at painting, I set myself to writing, to say the things I'd wanted to say through painting." Times have changed; today, Bowie is as embroiled in fine art as he is in rock. He's not only a patron, but a publisher, a critic and, most importantly, an exhibiting artist.

His interest in painting was aroused by a school art teacher. Owen Frampton's art classes encouraged freedom of expression, and David flourished under his master's direction, obtaining a rare O-level pass in the subject. His artistic flair was also felt at home where he painted cave-like images on the walls of his bedroom.

Frampton, whose guitar-playing son Peter was also destined for a musical career, helped David find his first job as a trainee graphic artist in a West End advertising agency. He lasted six months. Making teas and performing menial tasks

killed off his enthusiam. Pop stardom, which would give him control and fame, proved far more appealing. When that failed, and he was taken under the wing of a new manager, Ken Pitt. Bowie's enthusiasm for art was reawakened by Pitt's enthusiasm for Aubrey Beardsley and the late Victorians.

But the great revelation came when he discovered Andy Warhol. Warhol worked

with the shiny surfaces of consumer society, like soup cans and tins of Coke. But he also magnified modern horrors, like the electric chair, car crashes, the media's desire to see grief. Even more intriguing was Warhol's persona, as blank as a plain canvas. It was possibly his greatest work of all.

Fulham, 1995, with samples of his work (*clockwise from left*): *Little Stranger, Metal Hearth And The Black Coat*, 1993; *The Crowd Pleasers*, 1978; *The Remember II*, 1995; *Ancestor*, 1995.

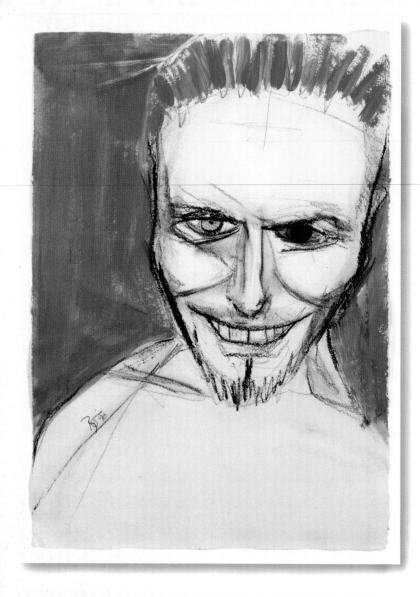

Walter Gramattè's 1921 canvas, *Selbstbildnis in Hiddensoe*, was the partial inspiration for Bowie's "*Heroes*" album sleeve.

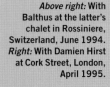

UNTITLED
low res. print/pea
MAC
from orig.
in acrylic

1999 ABSOLUT SECRET

1326

Above: Bowie recently revamped *The Crowd Pleasers* as a unique postcard piece for a Royal College of Art exhibition where the identity of the artist is only revealed on the reverse after purchase. Price? Just £35

The more Bowie read about modern art, the more he realised that rock was still in the dark ages. Picasso and Dali had confounded audiences with sudden changes in style and flagrant self-promotion decades ago. Art had proved powerful enough to withstand the anti-art strategies of the Dadaists and Surrealists, whose visual time-bombs had threatened to make art irrelevant. All these issues thrilled Bowie, and helped shape the intellectual backdrop to his work in the early Seventies. Bowie always doodled – Radio 1 producer Jeff Griffin remembers him sketching a Ziggy-inspired *The*

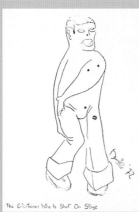

The Entertainer Who Is Shot On Stage

Entertainer Who Is Shot On Stage during a 1972 recording session. But it was while filming *The Man Who Fell To Earth* in 1975, when Bowie had time on his hands and a barren, New Mexico sagebrush desert to contemplate, that he began sketching in earnest. By the time of his 1976 tour, he carried a sketch-book everywhere.

his thirst for art had become all-consuming. He continued to paint, buried himself in text-books and artists' monographs, began investing in little-known contemporary works, and was a frequent visitor to the Brucke Museum Of Expressionist Art in West Berlin. Two paintings in the Brücke collection inspired album sleeves: Erich Heckel's *Roquairol* provided the model for Iggy Pop's engaging pose on his Bowie-assisted 1977 album, *The Idiot*; while the similarly-angular poise of Gramatté's self-portrait was adopted by Bowie for his "*Heroes*" album. A third, Otto Mueller's intense, eerily prescient *Lovers Between Garden Walls* (this was Berlin, remember), was an inspiration for the title track. Bowie's art aspirations – and connections – became more fully realised during the Nineties.

In 1993, he joined the board of the quarterly magazine *Modern Painters*; where he's contributed articles and reviews on various subjects, including Tracey Emin, Julian Schnabel and Jeff Koons (*with Bowie, above*), African art and a 12,000 word piece on Balthus. He's courted the BritArt generation,

Above right: With Balthus at the latter's chalet in Rossiniere, Switzerland, June 1994. *Right:* With Damien Hirst at Cork Street, London, April 1995.

particularly Damien Hirst, (*above*) with whom he collaborated on some 'spin art' (*right*). He is also a director of 21, a publishing company specialising in fine art books. Titles so far include artist/critic Matthew Collings' *Blimey!* and William Boyd's biography of fictitious artist Nat Tate.

Bowie first exhibited a whole series of artworks in 1994 when *We Saw A Minotaur* was included as part of *Little Pieces From Big Stars*, a fund-raising collection of celebrity art. In April 1995, The Gallery In Cork Street mounted his first one-man show, *New Afro/Pagan And Work 1975-1995*, a retrospective that included Expressionist-influenced figurative work, sculptures and computer-generated wallpaper designs. The majority of the collection was sold (one piece fetched a respectable £17,500), prompting a second show in Basle, Switzerland the following year. Since then, Bowie has become increasingly enthralled by computer-generated images, which he now sells via his BowieArt website.

For all the talk of media cross-pollinisation, critics have found Bowie's fine art aspirations difficult to take. Statements like "I'm a mid-art populist and postmodernist Buddhist who is casually surfing his way through the chaos of the late 20th century" are probably not the best way to mollify his detractors. According to his agent Kate Chertavian, these suspicions are misplaced: "I think his credibility grows with each year and each successful project that he does." She maintains that his work will endure, "partly because he is one of the first to cross mediums like this successfully."

Portrait of the artist in four parts. 1996 Self Portraits, available from www.bowieart.com.

Damien Hirst and David Bowie... beautiful, hello, space-boy painting, 1995.

Before venturing into the cultish world of R&B, and the dandified universe of the Mod, David cut his musical teeth with a local covers band, The Kon-rads. Early publicity shots show the group smartly turned out in matching suits and ties, the kind of budget sophisticate look favoured by the pre-pop dance combos. David, strikingly blond and with an immaculate DA (duck's arse) hairstyle, was the band's frontman and visual focus, despite being the most inexperienced member.

By early 1963, he was sporting a fashionable Beatle cut, encouraging the band to consider their presentation (apparently he suggested they wear zoot suits or Wild West outfits) and writing his own songs. Clearly, he had outgrown the passé and formula-ridden Kon-rads. Instead, he began raiding Carnaby Street dustbins for expensive Italian cast-offs, and threw his lot in with the hard-edged music emerging from the London clubs.

Rhythm & Blues (R&B), a bi-product of the jazz scene, was the biggest musical undercurrent in 1963, and a dominant commercial force over the next two years thanks to the success of groups like The Rolling Stones, The Animals, The Yardbirds and Them. More than a musical style, R&B was a mission; its followers were zealots, usually disaffected young men who envied the success of The Beatles and the Mersey groups, but regarded them with suspicion.

In adopting the music, attitude and argot of the American black man, the white suburban blue boys occupied the cultural high ground. Beatle-mania was loveable, moptoppish and ubiquitous. R&B was its surly, shabbier cousin, who preferred to be on the outside looking in.

For the next year or so, David Jones invested in a pair of casual trousers and waistcoat and immersed himself in R&B. Less concerned with debates about purism and 'authenticity' (he favoured the newer jazz/soul flavours over the founding fathers from Chicago and the Mississippi Delta), he fronted a succession of bands (Dave's Reds & Blues, The Hooker Brothers) looking every inch the Brian Jones (Rolling Stones) or Keith Relf (Yardbirds) wannabe.

After a couple of false starts, David joined The King Bees, whose lone 1964 single, 'Liza Jane', got lost amid the great R&B goldrush. The experience did allow him to indulge his passion for fashion, though, and as king of The King Bees, 'Davie' augmented the standard waistcoat and high-collared shirt look with a bizarre pair of calf-length suede boots. The dandification didn't stop there: he wore several rings, a brightly-coloured cravat and sported a layered haircut that virtually doubled the size of his head.

Within months, this gnome-like apparition had been replaced by the full 'Keith Relf'. The long blond bob was far more flattering to his chiselled features, framing his classic face in the manner of a Swinging Sixties 'dolly bird'. It was a look that would have tested the patience of every hair-dresser, and aroused the wrath of the spotty beer boys on every street corner.

Now vocalist with The Manish Boys, David had been 'made' President of the International League For The Preservation Of Animal Filament, later the Society For The Prevention of Cruelty To Long-Haired Men, a publicity scam arranged by his agent. It got his name in the papers, complaining that "anyone who has the courage to wear his hair down to his shoulders has to go through hell", and on television, where he told Tonight presenter Cliff Michelmore: "For the last two years, we've had comments like 'darling' and 'Can I carry your handbag?' thrown at us and I think it has to stop.

In one 1964 interview, David insisted, "I would sooner achieve the status as a Manish Boy that Mick Jagger enjoys as a Rolling Stone than end up a small-name solo singer." With his next group, The Lower Third, he had it both ways, adding his name as the prefix. Impatient and still desperately chasing success, he modelled the group on The Who, hitching mid-Sixties Carnaby Street Mod imagery to a more metropolitan take on R&B. The group's first single, 'You've Got A Habit Of Leaving', was a clear appropriation of The Who's sound; they'd even roped in Who producer Shel Talmy for the session.

As David's pop modernist styles grew ever more flamboyant, his hipster strides, chisel-toed shoes and highly-cultivated (and lacquered)

The Mannish Boys in Maidstone's Mote Park, 1964: "It's all criminals round there. It's the only time in my life I've ever been beaten up. This big herbert just knocked me on the pavement, and proceeded to kick the shit out of me. I haven't got many good memories of Maidstone."

INFLUENCES AND HEROES

Elvis Presley

"I saw a cousin of mine dance when I was very young. She was dancing to Elvis's 'Hound Dog' and I had never seen her get up and be moved so much by anything. It really impressed me, the power of music." The 12-year-old David Jones told a school-teacher that he intended to become "the British Elvis" – with whom he shared the same birthday, 8 January.

Terry Burns

David's elder half brother was handsome, image-conscious and, unlike his younger sibling, always at odds with the Jones family. He introduced David to beat books, jazz and philosophy, but his descent into schizo-phrenia, which became an enduring motif in Bowie's work (most notably on 'All The Madmen' and 'The Bewlay Brothers'), ended in his suicide in 1985 ,inspiring another song, 'Jump They Say'. "I saw so little of him and I think I unconsciously exaggerated his importance for me," David said in 1993. "I invented this hero-worship to discharge my guilt and failure, and to set myself free from my own hang-ups."

In the card that accompanied his funeral bouquet, Bowie wrote "You've seen more things than we could imagine..."

Lindsay Kemp

Ken Pitt introduced Bowie to bourgeois art forms. In 1967-68, maverick dancer Lindsay Kemp, who'd trained under mime master Marcel Marceau, invited Bowie into a more relaxed world that revolved around the Dance Centre in Covent Garden. There, Bowie learned about make-up, bodily control and flamboyant characters, the likes of whom he'd not come across in pop circles. "Wonderful, incredible," said Bowie years later. "The whole thing was so excessively French, with Left Bank existentialism, reading Genet and listening to R&B. The perfect Bohemian life."

Anthony Newley

One decidedly strange interlude during Bowie's long march to discovering his 'true' voice was the appropriation of the mannered Mockney style of old-school showbiz star Anthony Newley. His 1967 debut album might just as well have been titled Bowie Sings Tony. "Yes, we have another Tony Newley here alright," quipped a New Musical Express reviewer.

Jacques Brel

Bowie discovered Belgian chanson singer Jacques Brel in 1967 via a tribute record put together by Mort Schuman. Brel's 'My Death'

was a regular fixture in Bowie's set between 1969 and 1973, by which time it was fully integrated into the Ziggy schema. Another Brel song, 'Port Of Amsterdam', was released as a B-side in 1973; meanwhile, Ziggy's famous "You're not alone" denouement was also Brel-inspired.

Scott Walker

The errant Walker Brothers frontman, who broke up the band and embarked on a genuinely enigmatic solo career, proved to Bowie that taking musical risks didn't necessarily mean following the latest underground fad. Walker covered Brel songs, littered his lyrics with cultured and cinematic references and, David admitted in 1993, dated one of Bowie's early girlfriends. Black Tie White Noise includes a version of Scott's 'Nite Flights', from an LP inspired by Bowie's 'Heroes'.

Mick Jagger

Bowie has always had sneaking admiration for the Rolling Stones frontman, a master of disguises whose ability to move with the times provides the template for rock'n'roll longevity. Jagger's white Mr. Fish frock, elegantly worn at the Stones' Hyde Park show in 1969, pre-empted Bowie's "man's

Tony Visconti recalls Bolan's brief (*below*) contribution to 'London Bye Ta Ta': "Just before David sings, "I loved her, I loved her," there's a very high, whining guitar - that's Marc."

Marc Bolan
Bowie wasn't the only ex-Mod wannabe from an unfashionable corner of London to alter the course of British rock during the early Seventies.

His companion and sometime rival was T. Rex mainman Marc Bolan, whose revivalist rock'n'roll riffs, flamboyant, look-at-me costumes and extravagant persona, provided a template for David to meddle with. Between 1968 and 1970, they shared producer, Tony Visconti, but 'officially' collaborated on record in just one day when Marc played guitar on Bowie's 'The Prettiest Star' and 'London Bye Ta Ta'. After a period of intense rivalry, the pair were briefly reunited for an appearance on Bolan's TV show in 1977, before Marc was killed in a car crash a week later. Bowie has occasionally performed Bolan's work, duetting with Morrissey on 'Cosmic Dancer' and in 1999 with Placebo for '20th Century Boy'.

dress". (David attended the open-air gig where he heard 'Space Oddity' previewed over the PA). Mick's brilliant, persona-skipping character in *Performance* (1968), anticipated the role-playing riddles of Ziggy et al.

Ray Davies
The influence of the Kinks' frontman, especially his well-observed vignettes of London life, cannot be underestimated. Bowie ended *Pin Ups* with a poignant version of Davies' 'Where Have All The Good Times Gone', and also acknowledged The Kinks' 'All Day And All Of The Night' on a 1996 tour.

Syd Barrett
Beautiful, terrifyingly gifted and blessed with the bittersweet curse of tragedy, Pink Floyd's original songwriter might have been dismissive about Bowie's 'Love You Till Tuesday' single ("I don't think my toes were tapping at all") in a magazine review, but his sharp fall from grace no doubt provided valuable source material for Ziggy Stardust. Barrett's lyrics drew on mysticism, space travel, social observation and an unhealthy dose of childish whimsy, mirrored those of the late Sixties Bowie. David covered Barrett's 1967 Pink Floyd hit, "See Emily Play", on *Pin Ups* in 1973.

Buddha
Bowie's interest in this Eastern philosophy has been dismissed as little more than a fad by Angie Bowie and Ken Pitt, but references continue to find their way into his work. Buddhism's most enduring legacy on Bowie may have impacted on a subconscious level. Reincarnation, the exchange of one identity for another, is a Buddhist belief. By tearing his mortal self apart at regular intervals, it could be said that Bowie was merely accelerating the process.

ALL THE OLD DUDES

Top: Warwick Square, 1966. "I prefer to observe London from the outside, and to write about it."

"There were some good tailors. The one I used to go to was the same one that Marc Bolan used to go to, a fairly well-known one in Shepherd's Bush. I remember I saved up and got one suit made there.
"I didn't really have a hangout for clothes. I didn't wear much that was fashionable, actually. I was quite happy with things like Fred Perrys and a pair of slacks."

Rehearsals for *Ready Steady Go!* with The Buzz, March 1966. The jacket was part of a "beautiful suit that I had made at Burtons. A tweed job, double-breasted with an Edwardian feel to it," Bowie recalls.

bouffant just one step ahead of the adventurous pack, he became increasingly frustrated by failure. The Lower Third gave way to The Buzz in 1966, but with no appreciable change in fortunes, David sacked them before the year was out citing financial difficulties. The nearest he got to stardom was going to gigs in his manager's Mark 10 Jaguar.

But help was at hand. In September 1965, David's then manager Ralph Horton was discussing his client with Ken Pitt, who'd been instrumental in the success of Manfred Mann a year or two earlier. Pitt advised him that with several David Jones's already struggling to find a foothold in the business, including one young Mancunian soon to find fame with The Monkees, Horton's charge ought to consider a name change. He'd briefly called himself Dave Jay during The Kon-rads days, but for this do-or-die change, he instead delved back to his schoolboy fascination for the Wild West and came up with a name derived from a popular hunting knife used by Jim Bowie, a hero at the battle of the Alamo. From now on, he would be known as David Bowie.

With the male answer to the Dusty Springfield beehive up top, the artist formerly known as Jones looks to possible solo success. Some claim the change was also inspired by a mysterious uncle already blessed with the Bowie name.

MICK ROCK

Bowie, pictured with photographer Mick Rock, in July 1973: "David has developed a true sense of his own mystique. He makes a fascinating study."

Mick Rock's photographs chronicled the crucial months during 1972 and '73, when Ziggy Stardust and Aladdin Sane exploded onto the world stage. He was the only cameraman allowed inside the Bowie camp on a regular basis during this era.

"The visual thing is what established him, the outrageousness of the costumes. My famous picture of him biting Mick Ronson's guitar, which they ran as a full page ad in *Melody Maker*, got seen all over the place so that helped a lot. When I first met David, in February 1972 during the early stages of Ziggy Stardust, his image was very different from what it became at the end when it was super-sophisticated. He'd just got the hairdo done. It was more blond then, more his own colour, but it wasn't long before it became the red that we know and love.

"Clearly he caught the zeitgeist in some interesting way. David is super bright but he's also extremely intuitive about people and ideas. By the summer, after Ziggy had taken off, he was already producing Lou Reed and Mott The Hoople and he was hustling Iggy around. He became influential very quickly, not just in rock'n'roll terms but in the wider culture. I don't think you could say he planned it all; he was like a force of nature. David is a very positive thinker, and always has been, even in his darkest hours. "Something happened to him around the time I met him and it galvanised everyone around him, me included. I art

directed the *Pin Ups* album and put together the promo films for 'John, I'm Only Dancing', 'Life On Mars?', 'Space Oddity' and 'The Jean Genie'. I was a bit of a Josef Goebbels at the time! David had a very empathetic way that made him inspire others. I mean, people still talk about *Transformer* and *Raw Power* and *All The Young Dudes* as being the most significant albums in the careers of those three acts. David was the centrifugal force that drove this magic moment in time.

"It was all done on a shoestring with smoke and mirrors. They rarely spent much money on it, not in the early days. The illusion was of this massive star, looking and acting like a star, and suddenly he became that. Marc Bolan was cute and big and got there first, but he didn't have the range and power that David had, or his intellect. David had great music and great visual appeal; he was ridiculously glamorous. Eventually, I think it started to exceed his wildest dreams. He sang about being a star before he was one; that's all over the *Ziggy Stardust* album. Before that, no one was interested, especially in England. That's why the *Hunky Dory* deal was done in America.

"The photo sessions were all very different. I got some great performance shots because he always looked so fantastic. I actually wasn't very good at live pictures because I'd not done much of that before David, but it was through him that I got good. There was so much stylised behaviour in his performance that he was great to shoot. It was like

watching a kaleidoscope; he just kept changing on stage.

"Taking the pictures happened very fast. There was very little planning; it was all action, all about interchange and interplay, a fast-paced intuitive thing. The control of the look was not contrived. It simply amounted to not letting photographers in so that they wanted to come in even more! I think he was the first to play that one, and I became part of the game. I was the exclusive photographer because no one else was really interested at the time. Then all that changed and it became, 'Only Mick Rock can shoot him'. And that worked very well.

"I had no warning for that fellatio shot, which I took at Oxford Town Hall in June 1972 (*right*). I was at the front of the stage, and when I moved to side, David suddenly did it. I remember him coming off stage and saying, 'Did you get it, did you get it?' I didn't know if it was planned or spontaneous, but he was always looking for a move that would break through. That one really did!

"I developed the shots the next morning, and took them round to the GEM office. David and Tony picked out the shot they liked best and rushed it off to the printers. They both knew it was a master image. They bought a page in *Melody Maker* and ran it like a fan advert. Looking back, it's a bit like Jimi Hendrix lighting his guitar or Pete Townshend smashing his up. David might regard that photo as being one of the key images of his career. It certainly made a dramatic and controversial statement.

"Androgyny was in the air and David was undoubtedly the finest manifestation of that. It was an innate part of his personality. If truth be told, David is very much a boy – I know a lot of girls he had sex with! But he would play up like English schoolboys do, groping and romping in the playground. You don't get that in America; it's very English. He developed that, and it became part of him.

"He loved the camera when that wasn't the ethic of the time. David would give you what you wanted, he was always up for it. I was able to work off that, but I wasn't allowed to photo Marc Bolan 'cos he and David weren't talking at the time. Marc wanted me to do stuff for him and wanted to stick his finger up to David! When they were younger, they were close for a long time, then something went wrong. When David got big, he then felt generous towards Marc.

"He's always up to something, even today. He never sits still; he's got an enormous amount of energy. He's still in control of his image, but also now his destiny. He used to be very passive about the business side, but now he gets very involved. Once he'd sign anything without reading it, but he's learnt from his mistakes."

Facing page: Going Down I, with Mick Ronson, a seminal moment in rock history. "I'm very into shock tactics. I want to stretch people and get a reaction. I don't think there's any point in doing anything artistically unless it astounds," Bowie announced.

1.3

Renaissancemanbowie

In 1967, Bowie put the youthful experiments with jazz, R&B and the Mod scene behind him. He placed himself under the tutelage of manager Ken Pitt, broadened his artistic horizons paying scant attention to contemporary trends and began to forge a new individualism. Their relationship, lovingly chronicled in Pitt's book, *The Pitt Report*, was, in the singer's estimation, "Pygmalion-like, to a certain extent". Bowie came to Pitt a battle-scarred young man, knocked back by three years of professional failure. He left a pop star, secure enough in his own abilities that he could step out of the limelight until the conditions for a more enduring success looked more favourable. It was, he said later, his "apprenticeship period".

Posterity has not always been kind to Pitt's role. Many feel he was out of his depth in the rapidly changing market, where muscular managers like Peter Grant (Led Zeppelin) and Allen Klein (The Beatles, The Rolling Stones) kept their noses out of their clients' creative affairs, concentrating instead on the aggressive pursuit of money, security and more money. Bowie's ex-wife Angie dismisses Pitt's desire to mould Bowie into a "Judy Garland for the rock generation", forgetting that during the early Seventies Bowie became almost exactly that. Under Pitt, Bowie affected an exaggerated Cockney voice as if he aspired to become the Tommy Steele or Anthony Newley of the Love Generation. Perhaps so, but Pitt's encouragement and dedication to the idea of creating an intellectually adept, multi-skilled pop star provided the basis for Bowie's future success.

Bowie's thirst for intellectual nourishment wasn't wholly created by Pitt, though. His aspirations beyond fashion and pop fame were evident as early as February 1966 when *Melody Maker* printed 'A Message To London From Dave': "I want to act. I'd like to do character parts. I think it

takes a lot to become somebody else; it takes some doing... As far as I'm concerned, the whole idea of Western life – that's the life we live now – is wrong. These are hard concepts to put into song, though." A contemporary press release echoes the change in visual terms: "Gone are the outlandish clothes, the long hair, and the wild appearance and instead we find a quiet talented vocalist and songwriter in David Bowie."

When Pitt first clasped eyes on Bowie, after a Marquee Club performance in April 1966, the effect was immediate: "His burgeoning charisma was undeniable but I was particularly struck by the artistry with which he used his body, as if it were an accompanying instrument, essential to the singer and the song." He also recognised Bowie's innate intellect and wanted to nurture it.

In June 1967, as his debut LP was issued, Bowie announced, "I'd like to write a musical. And really the ultimate would be to have one or two of my songs become standards, and used by artistes like Frank Sinatra."

Facing page: In paisley. "Aah, this is sweet. It was taken in around '67. I was 20. I look very young, very fresh -faced. There's a bit of a psychedelic shirt going on as well."

GAY GAMES

This European CD of Sixties recordings, with an alternative slate grey dress shot from The Man Who Sold The World photo sessions, appeared in 1995.

Right: Liverpool, June 1973, in Pelican shoes with palm tree motif. "Oh, it was fab. The best show ever." - Holly Johnson.

Below: Camp David. At Santa Monica, October 1972. Michael Watts: "David's present image is to come on like a swishy queen, a gorgeously effeminate boy. He's as camp as a row of tents with his limp hand and trolling vocabulary."

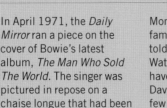

In April 1971, the *Daily Mirror* ran a piece on the cover of Bowie's latest album, *The Man Who Sold The World*. The singer was pictured in repose on a chaise longue that had been draped in blue velvet. He was wearing what he called his "man's dress". Countering the paper's barely-concealed prurience, Bowie insisted that he was "not queer and all sorts of things... my sexual life is normal".

Bowie's "I'm Gay" declaration in January 1972 was the master-stroke that secured his career. "Best thing I ever said, I suppose," he later confessed. But there were reservations: *NME*'s Charles Shaar Murray lamented the fact that "it took a spate of calculatedly outrageous acts to bring him any reasonable degree of mass recognition". Of course it was a shameless act of hype, and all the more bizarre considering his family man status – he was married with a small son – and keen appetite for groupies, most of whom were hot-blooded women.

Nevertheless, in a rock world where homosexuality was barely acknowledged, his comments broke one of the last taboos. "As soon as your article came out," Bowie told Watts months later, "people rang up and

Going Down II: Ronno comes under erotic attack during 'Cracked Actor', Earl's Court, May 1973.

Months later, in his most famous interview ever, Bowie told *Melody Maker*'s Michael Watts: "I'm gay and I always have been, even when I was David Jones." Over the next few years, matters of his sexual orientation were flirted with but left open to interpretation. But in 1976, Bowie confessed all to *Playboy* magazine, revealing a deep-seated bisexuality: "It didn't really matter who or what it was with, as long as it was a sexual experience. So it was some very pretty boy in class in some school or other that I took home and neatly fucked on my bed upstairs." After 1979, the one-time "King Of Camp Rock" remained remarkably elusive on the subject, though in recent years he's often referred to himself as a "closet heterosexual".

said, 'Don't buy the paper. You know what you've gone and done? You've just ruined yourself.' They said, 'You told him you were bisexual.' I said, I know, he asked me! Nobody is going to be offended by that; everybody knows that most people are bisexual." Unfortunately, despite the proliferation of unisex hairdressers and boutiques, they didn't.

There was an inevitable backlash. Readers wrote in expressing their fears for what might become a new genre ("Fag-Rock", suggested one), and speculated whether they might yet see Elvis in drag. *Music Scene* took a pot-shot at what it called "The Powder-Puff Bandwagon"; noted US critic Lester Bangs unleashed reams of bile about "faggot rock"; *Newsday*'s Robert Christgau questioned whether "songs about Andy Warhol written by an English fairy (were) enough for American audiences". *Disc* asked 'Why Bowie Is Feeling Butch'. *Sounds* couldn't resist a few playful innuendos, claiming that Bowie's Rainbow show "didn't quite come off", and quoting Elton John saying he thought Bowie had "blown it". After *Melody Maker* made *Ziggy Stardust* the best album of 1972, one reader complained that the paper was "now fawning at and licking the boots (covered in silver glitter of course), of a drag artist... If this is the best album of the year in your coveted opinion, then

what are we to expect as your 1973 choice – *Shirley Temple's Greatest Hits*? God help rock."

Sections of the gay press were also suspicious of Bowie's freak show bisexuality, though the emerging lesbian and gay movement generally welcomed the fact that the issue was at least on the agenda. Writing in July 1972, *Gay News'* Peter Holmes was hopeful: "David Bowie is probably the best rock musician in Britain now. One day, he'll become as popular as he deserves to be. And that'll give gay rock a potent spokesman." A year later, the same magazine anticipated Bowie's Earl's Court show with a cover story that claimed: "17,000 of us will be there!"

The publicity served Bowie well. He fanned the debate by adopting an increasingly androgynous look, and showing a keen interest in costume and theatre. But the pop news story of 1972 was encapsulated in a single photograph: Mick Rock's shot of Bowie on his knees and 'fellating' Mick Ronson's guitar was quickly distributed and has since become the defining image of Glam Rock. Fans who scoured

Edinburgh, May 1973. Twenty years later he recalled his *Melody Maker* interview: "I had been bisexual for many years before I made that statement but it was perceived like it was a great gimmick. I found out I wasn't truly a bisexual but I loved the flirtation with it, I enjoyed the excitement of being involved in an area that had had been perceived as a social taboo. That excited me a lot."

Bowie's lyrics for further
clues discovered plenty of
references to an uncertain
sexuality, some dating back
to his 1967 LP. In Spain, one
Bowie album was titled *El
Ray Del Gay Power*.

Bowie's arrival certainly
broadened the palette of
role-models for a generation
of pop fans, and many
prominent gay celebrities
have since described the
liberating effect Bowie had
in unlocking their true
sexuality. Ultimately, though,
Bowie's personal sexual
ambivalence might better be
understood in the wider
context of his work. It has
more to do with the
aesthetics of camp than
being gay. "Camp sees
everything in quotation
marks," wrote Susan Sontag.
"It is the fullest extension, in
sensibility, of the metaphor
of life as theatre." And, as
Sontag states in her 'Notes
On Camp' essay: "The
androgyne is certainly one of
the great images of Camp
sensibility."

In 1993, Bowie reflected:
"I don't think I did anything
that my contemporaries didn't;
it was just that I was the
only one who talked about it.
In the Sixties anyone who had a
sense of style seemed to be gay.
I wanted to identify with that."

Pierrot In Turquoise at London's Mercury Theatre, March 1968. The show's designer Natasha Kornilof recalls: "Silk organza! That big ruff was pink and maroon and I wound it twice around his neck, this amazing collar. He's a good clothes hanger."

To that end, he installed Bowie into his Manchester Street flat, a tasteful bachelor-pad filled with classic literature and paintings. Pitt's social circle was markedly different to anything David had known. Laddish colleagues and eager girl fans were replaced by showbiz impresarios and restaurateurs, record company bosses and theatrical agents. Bowie was encouraged to consider a theatrical career, to which end Pitt accompanied him to several top London productions, including Lionel Bart's *Oliver!* and *Aladdin*, starring Cliff Richard. And he was exposed to the European chanson tradition, via the work of Jacques Brel, who'd also been picked up on by renegade Walker Brother Scott Walker. When he wasn't dressed up for his mime performances with Lindsay Kemp, or in squaddie uniform for a minuscule film role in *The Virgin Soldiers*, Bowie often resembled a young Walker during these years – smart but hip, serious and often dressed in dark clothes.

Threepenny Pierrot.
"It was an important transitional period. Mime doesn't need words."

Pitt's wide-angled view on pop artistry, coupled with the flourishing arts scene that took off in the wake of the 1967 hippie revolution, encouraged Bowie to look beyond songwriting. That was just as well because Pitt had been unable to secure him a new deal after Bowie's 1967 LP flopped. Instead, David busied himself at Lindsay Kemp's mime classes, playing the role of Cloud in Kemp's *Pierrot In Turquoise* during a short national tour. He wrote plays and discussed film projects with budding directors. Early in 1969, Pitt financed a 30-minute film, *Love You Till Tuesday*, ostensibly to parade his multi-skilled client. Just one thing was missing: a new song. David came up with 'Space Oddity'.

Released, but not written, to coincide with the Moon landing, 'Space Oddity' didn't take off untill late in the year, just weeks after the death of David's father. Both events hastened Pitt's demise. Since 1967, the world had changed immeasurably, and in ways that Pitt, a gentleman aesthete with a passion for late Victorian *fin de siecle* culture and a mistrust of the TV generation, could never quite accept. (When Bowie adopted a shaggy, Bob Dylan-style perm, in anticipation of his raised public profile, the disappointed Pitt saw only "a failed Afro".) Success meant that Bowie now had as much to lose as to gain; his apprenticeship was over.

In spring 1970, Bowie cast his old 'mentor' aside, and put himself in the hands of new manager Tony DeFries and his wife and greatest cheerleader Angie. No longer duty-bound to maintain a peaceable status quo with a father-figure, Bowie embraced the contemporary spirit with a vengeance: sex, drugs, flamboyance, indecency, everything, in fact, that would have offended Pitt's more traditional sensibilities.

Above left, October, 1968, Ken Pitt: "He was going to Elstree to do what little bit he had to do for *The Virgin Soldiers* (Bowie appears briefly behind the bar during a fight scene). I thought we could exploit the situation. I had to get some pictures of him in the uniform, so I asked him to smuggle it home one day. I took this shot at his flat in Clareville Grove."
Above right: "This was taken the night before having his hair shorn for the role."

"Arts labs should be for everybody - not just the so-called turned-on minority… we need energy from all directions, heads and skinheads alike."

Bowie listed his loves in December 1969, which included, "Zany clothes - especially my space suit, which is of genuine space material and is warm in winter, cool in summer."

Facing page: 'Hole In The Ground' is a little-known track which didn't make it on to Bowie's eponymously-titled 1969 LP.

The July 1969 moon landing provided topical, and hardly unexpected, publicity for 'Space Oddity', though it would be several months before the single charted.

Success finally came Bowie's way when 'Space Oddity', a memorable slice of cosmic folk whimsy, broke into the British Top 5 in November 1969. The record had been released in July to coincide with the imminent Moon landing, but topical songs – and their singers – rarely enjoy a long shelf-life. Ken Pitt believed it was merely the first of many giant steps, but to most observers David Bowie had "one-hit wonder" written all over his classically proportioned features.

Bowie seized his moment. He attended music industry showcases on the continent, endorsed a "pocket electronic organ" called the Stylophone, oiled the publicity machine with interviews and photo-shoots, and promoted the record on tour. Fame had always been

Bowie's goal, and he took his role as a late Sixties Starman seriously. He acquired a curly perm, a nod in the direction of hippie fashion, but one which was also being adopted by mainstream groups like Marmalade and The Herd. The 1969 pop audience would have found it difficult to discern any difference between David Bowie and the next hopeful in loose-fitting silk shirt and hipster trousers.

The downside of his new-found fame was that 'Space Oddity' threatened to over-whelm him. In a live review titled "Up-To-Date Minstrel", in December 1969, *The Observer's* Tony Palmer wrote: "I realised that Major Tom had stolen his creator's thunder, that in the public's mind he was the star of the show, not David Bowie." To

the star-in-waiting, to be eclipsed by one of his own creations was a great blow. When it happened again, in 1972, he made sure that no one was left in any doubt who the star was.

Bowie had drifted aimlessly in a pop market that refused to take him seriously. The rock scene preferred groups. When Anne Nightingale suggested early in 1970 that he could become a big romantic star like Scott Walker, David replied: "I don't relish the idea of that kind of stardom very much". His good looks and natural charm made him an obvious successor to the 'Face Of 68' Peter Frampton, and winning 'Best Newcomer' and 'Brightest Hope' (*below right, with Cliff Richard*) in music paper polls at the end of the year suggested great things.

Bowie chose a different path. In spring 1970, in a piece titled 'A New Star Shoots Upwards', he told *Disc* magazine's Penny Valentine that his "own ambitions come before any career as such". He'd already flirted with the guise of the hippie singer-songwriter the previous summer, organising a series of 'happenings' at the Beckenham Arts Lab and an open-air festival. Now he was turning his back on stardom. It was a belated sop to the counterculture, but Bowie wasn't convinced by the gurus of anti-materialism, telling *Music Now!* magazine how much he liked money and how he despised those "hypocritical" groups who espoused the new creed but chased success all the same. Like some character in the French Revolution, Bowie seemed to have kept his

In his putty-coloured "special event suit", at the Cafe Royal, Valentine's Day 1970. "Wasn't particularly pleased to meet Cliff. I was never a great fan of his." For an album in 1993, Cliff would record the 'Space Oddity' countdown on Hank Marvin's cover of the song.

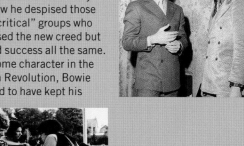

"Ah, the Stylophone! Marc Bolan gave me that one. He said, 'You like this kind of stuff, do something with it'. I put it on 'Space Oddity', so it served me well. It was just a little signal responding to electrodes. Sounded atrocious. The idea here was that if I did a promotion, then they'd give me a whole bunch of them."

At the Beckenham Free Festival. "With 'Space Oddity', I went out in front of these gum-chewing skinheads. As soon as I appeared, looking a bit like Bob Dylan with this curly hair and denims, I was whistled at and booed. At one point I had cigarettes thrown at me."

STARMAN : FIRST BITE

1.4

Dame Meditation

It says much for Bowie's chameleon-like tendencies that in 1967 *Chelsea News* was able to report that: "David is contented with contentment: he is a happy loving person with a gentle nature which reigns supreme over all agitation. He is the only person whom I have met who brings nursery rhymes and fairy stories to the foreground of my mind." In theory, he fitted perfectly the hippie stereotype, but with a bourgeois Svengali and a well-developed individuality that required no psychedelic enhancement, Bowie initially spurned the new underground.

In rejecting the Eastern-inspired and brightly coloured rock fashions of flower power, Bowie fell out of sync with the prevailing trends. Unlike Marc Bolan, who revelled in the exotic splendour of hippie elegance, Bowie found it difficult to reject his ingrained, upwardly mobile Mod sensibility for a look that ultimately amounted to a perversely anti-fashion, anti-materialist statement. Anyway, he thought, it won't last.

Bowie's continuing interest in Buddhism reveals itself in songs like 'Seven Years In Tibet'.

'Little Wonder', Bowie's self-deprecating 1997 single, made a great play on his flirtations with Buddhism thirty years before.

Even in 1967, hippie culture and David Bowie weren't complete enemies. His modest interest in Buddhism went into overdrive after The Beatles' venture to India, and though both Ken Pitt and Angie Bowie have since downplayed his commitment, contemporary records ('Silly Boy Blue', 'Karma Man') and interviews are peppered with references. Bowie once told journalist George Tremlett that he slept upright in a wooden box, ate two small meals a day and observed lengthy periods of silence, none of which Tremlett believed for a moment. But Bowie and his producer Tony Visconti did join the Tibet Society and briefly studied under a London-based Tibetan monk, Chime Rimpoche.

Facing page: With little-known band The Riot Squad in April 1967. "I inflicted my taste for the theatrical upon them. This was the first band I was in where make-up and interesting trousers were as important as the music. I wanted them to be the English Mothers Of Invention. The guy who did these photos was Gerald Fearnley, whose brother, Dek, played bass in The Buzz with me."

Bowie is fascinated by ancient mythological creatures. His 1995 artwork, *The Voyeur Of Utter Destruction As Beauty* (*below*) depicts the Minotaur. Twenty-five years before that it was Cyclops, which, as Tony Visconti recalls, "was the working title for 'The Supermen'. David said, "I'm gonna write a song about these big guys with one eye in the middle of their head. They're like supermen."

"I really believe that Bob Dylan (with Joan Baez, right) and others have speeded up the changes. Pacifism has found a voice at last." - Bowie '69

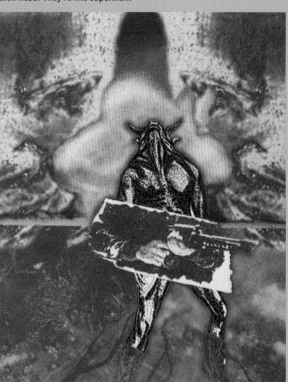

As he entered adulthood, these feelings intensified. 'Please Mr Gravedigger', a macabre tale about a child murderer, and 'We Are Hungry Men', which visualised an overpopulated world on the cusp of a catastrophe, were released during the year of love and peace. In fact, the melancholy man's reluctance to use psychedelic drugs is probably entwined in all this, fearing that this might stir demons that would be better left untroubled. It was confusing enough being a bystander with a fractured sense of identity without bringing acid into the equation.

Discussing the fate of the counter-culture in 1974 with Charles Shaar Murray, Bowie said, "I could never take all that seriously, because as you know, I'm an awful fatalist. I knew that nothing would happen… I'm pessimistic about new things, new projects, new ideas, as far as society's concerned. I think it's all over, personally. I think the end of the world happened ten years ago. This is it." This wasn't revisionism, either. One of Angie's first impresssions of David in 1969 was that "the paranoid vision and the language of life's darkness were second nature to him".

"Planet Earth is blue, and there's nothing I can do." It's a gorgeous hook, but that memorable line from 'Space Oddity' also betrays the pessimistic philosophies that have largely informed Bowie's world view. Today, without the crutch of a medicine cabinet and a retinue of imposing aides, David Bowie is the consummate gentleman. Even in the dark days of the mid-Seventies, he couldn't help but break into a chummy exterior. He tends to keep it well hidden these days, but beneath the conviviality and the masks lies a tangle of notions and theories that amount to a complete fascination for personal breakdown and social catastrophe.

"I thought I'd write my problems out," Bowie once said, thereby acknowledging the common bond between creativity and despair. His awareness of a family tendency towards mental illness was one of many factors that could have contributed to a disposition keenly attuned to the politics of fear and disaster. He wasn't alone: even the early Sixties' folk/protest boom, spearheaded by Joan Baez and Bob Dylan, was a response to the doomsday scenario of nuclear war. One of Bowie's first lyrics, according to an ex-Kon-rad colleague, was based on a news story about an air-crash ('I Never Dreamed'); another, 'Tired Of My Life', included the line, "Put a bullet in my brain / And I make all the papers", a neat foretaste of 'Rock'n'Roll Suicide'.

Bowie with Angie at
Victoria Station, 1973.

In recent years Bowie has played down the Aleister Crowley influence. "I'm always very suspicious of anybody who says they're into Crowley (*left*). 'Quicksand'? That's before I tried reading him, when I had his biography in my raincoat so the title showed. That was reading on the tube."

The late Sixties quest for alternative world views elevated the work of two iconoclasts, diabolist Aleister Crowley and philosopher Friedrich Nietzsche. Crowley, an Edwardian sinner who courted outrage and answered to the name of "The Great Beast", was a leading occultist who sought to liberate the subconscious mind through a mix of Magick and Oriental wisdom. Two neat soundbites resounded through the hippie hovels: "Do what thou wilt shall be the whole of the Law", and "Every man and every woman is a star". Those who looked a little harder found another: "Nothing is true; everything is permitted".

Bowie admired Crowley's work. "I'm closer to the Golden Dawn / Immersed in Crowley's uniform", he admitted on 1971's 'Quicksand'. Unfortunately, the tirade of self-doubt that followed suggested that Bowie wasn't ready to do what he wilt just yet. By 1975, though, fear had got the better of him. Allegedly, jars of urine lined his refrigerator in a bid to ward off evil spirits. *White Stains*, an obscure Crowley text, was namechecked on the album that followed, *Station To Station*.

Bowie also tipped his bipperty-boppity hat to Friedrich Nietzsche, the 19th century German thinker who famously declared that God was dead and advanced the cause of personal destiny. A 1970 song, 'The Supermen', was titled after Nietzsche's most famous – and controversial – concept. Nietzsche's

David Bowie and Lou Reed find each other again. Their gritty lyrical realism provided a notable contrast to the dewy-eyed romanticism of the Seventies prog-rock bards.

footsoldiers, Supermen were escapees from what the philosopher called "slave morality", who rejected the 'truth' of the prevailing moral order. The idea, which subsequently got twisted into Nazi ideology, was more about intellectual elitism; when Bowie sang "You gotta make way for the Homo Superior" on 'Oh! You Pretty Things' in 1971, it was part Nietzschean recognition part wish-fulfilment.

Bowie was attracted to Crowley and Nietzsche because he sought the truth, however disturbing it might be. In another song, 'Width Of A Circle', Bowie sang: "I ran across a monster who was sleeping by a tree / And I looked and frowned 'cos the monster was me". But Bowie, who'd begun to liken himself to a "photostat machine", saw his personal disintegration as a mirror to the world around him. "People like Lou (Reed) and I are probably predicting the end of an era and I mean that catastrophically," he said in 1972. "Any society that allows people like Lou and I to become rampant is pretty well lost."

The Rise And Fall element in *Ziggy Stardust* echoed doomed projects of social engineering like the Roman Empire or the Third Reich. Bowie became neurotic, insisting he wouldn't travel by plane or stay in a hotel room above the eighth floor. He also insisted he had "a strange… psychosomatic death-wish thing". Only after the murder of John Lennon in December 1980 did he appear to exorcise that particular line of self-emancipation, and adopt a more positive outlook.

The philosophy of Friedrich Nietzsche cast long shadows over the 20th century - and Bowie's work.

Facing page: Let Me Sleep Beside You. A bewigged David with Hermione on Hampstead Heath for the 'Love You Till Tuesday' film shoot, January 1969. The steel-grey suit (from Just Men by Nikki) was trimmed with electric blue braid, though when it turned up at auction in 1994, the braiding had been removed below the lapel. "That was because we'd had the jacket re-cut for him to wear at the Malta Song Festival in July of '69," Ken Pitt explains. The suit, together with the accompanying white ruffled dress shirt (by Bob Fletcher) fetched £2,000 at Christie's.

Left: A paint-splattered Ziggy doing some touching up to the high moulded ceilings at Haddon Hall. *Bottom left:* "Is that a rugby shirt? This was Beckenham Arts Lab. Very little happened at these 'happenings'. That's quite a perm I've got there. Not my greatest hairstyle."

Far left: With Dylanesque harmonica holder, obscuring bass-playing producer, Tony Visconti.

Left: A rare colour shot of Growth's Summer Festival and Free Concert at Beckenham Recreation Ground, August 1969. Songs played included Biff Rose's 'Buzz The Fuzz' and Cream's 'I Feel Free'.

Having nailed his mast to that of a cultured Eurocentric, only to discover that the peasants wanted to let it all hang out at American-style love-ins, Bowie entered the months of acid-inspired abandon with some reservation. Joining Lindsay Kemp's mime troupe owed little to the new-fangled hippie arts scene, although forming a mixed-media trio named Feathers, with girlfriend Hermione Farthingale and old pal John 'Hutch' Hutchinson, was certainly a very 1968 thing to do. By early '69 the experiment was over, and Bowie, by now "a combination of penniless art student and hard-core hippie" according to new girlfriend Angela Barnett, hitched a ride on the new singer-songwriter boom. He hoped to open a folk club in central London; instead, he was forced to settle for a back room in the Three Tuns pub in Beckenham High Street, a short walk from his parents' home.

Nominally styled an 'Arts Lab', the weekly event was essentially a showcase for Bowie, the intimate atmosphere giving him the opportunity to develop a rapport with the audience. He really began to dig it, as this uncharacteristic quote to underground freak-sheet *International Times* confirms: "I feel compassion as a source of energy; the individual is less important than the source of energy of which he is part."

This idyllic interlude climaxed in the Growth Festival, held in a Beckenham park on August 16, 1969, and immortalised on Bowie's 'Memory Of A Free Festival'. "We claimed the very source of joy ran through / It didn't, but it seemed that way," was his clear-eyed assessment of the event. Two years later, Bowie played the song at the Glastonbury Festival as dawn rose – but he'd never write another one like it again.

With girlfriend Angie as a protective buffer, Bowie confidently entered the spirit of collectivism in October 1969 when the pair moved into a ground floor flat in Beckenham. To the postman, it was plain old Flat 7, 42 Southend Rd., but to Angie, David and the many long and short-stay visitors they entertained there during the next three years, it was grandiosely referred to as Haddon Hall. With its stained glass windows, moulded ceilings, minstrel's gallery, tiled fireplaces, ornate lamps, Regency bed, velvet curtains and Oriental rugs it was the perfect post-*Sgt. Pepper* crash-pad, an oasis of cheaply purchased Victoriana and bric-a-brac.

The collision of a liberated, hippie-inspired way of life and a setting created out of bourgeois cast-offs was a Bohemian paradise. The Jones' family home was a short walk away, but culturally the distance was now immeasurable.

The Beckenham house husband with mop, but no bucket, at the front entrance to his new home. In the basement was the so-called Haddon Hall rehearsal studio, which, as Tony Visconti recalls, was really just "a wine cellar. It was a very small room, there was no real studio there."

The short-lived trio, Bowie, Farthingale and Hutchinson, in 1968. "I had absolutely no belief in Feathers at all," says Ken Pitt.

At the BBC's Paris Cinema Studios, February 1970: "We'd heard that David Bowie was supposed to be androgynous and everything, but then he came out with long hair, folky clothes, and sat on a stool and played folk songs. We were so disappointed with him. We looked over and said, 'Just look at that folky old hippy'." - Wayne County.

Despite a solo career that has seen more highs than most of his long-term contemporaries, Bowie has been involved in some dubious duets.

Cher
Bowie duetted with Cher on a 'Young Americans' medley, which took in seven standards along the way, and a version of 'Can You Hear Me' on her US TV show in 1975.

Mick Jagger
The spectacle of these two giants attempting to torch their reputations in just under four minutes of 1985's 'Dancing In The Street' wasn't the ideal incentive to donate money to alleviate the crisis in Ethiopia. Never allowing them near a studio together again seemed like a much better idea...

Placebo
With no album to promote, Bowie still managed to wing an appearance at the 1999 Brit Awards show by teaming up with Placebo for a version of T. Rex's '20th Century Boy'. They collaborated again at a New York show weeks later.

Bing Crosby
The absurdity of sharing a homely stage set with ancient crooner Bing Crosby for a medley of 'Peace On Earth' and 'Little Drummer Boy' almost prompted Bowie to crack on screen. A month later, Bing went Bong at the climax of a game of golf, and the collaboration, recorded to celebrate Christmas 1977, took five years to appear on record.

Marc Bolan
The only public appearance of the two Glam Rock luminaries took place on the final episode of Bolan's daytime TV show, *Marc*. Even then, the collaboration, 'Sitting Next To You' was hampered when filming overran and the plugs were pulled – but not before Bolan had toppled off the stage. It was a shambolic end to a competitive but mostly affectionate relationship, because days later, in the early hours of September 16, 1977, Bolan was killed in a car crash in Barnes, West London.

Queen

The Eighties began in earnest for David when he teamed up with Queen in 1981 for the soft-metal anthem, 'Under Pressure'. The bassline provided the hook, the vocal sparrings the talking-point. The record was a great success at home, but the most enduring aspect of the collaboration was Freddie Mercury's (*above, backstage with Bowie at Live Aid*) suggestion that Bowie might be happier at EMI than he had been at RCA. When Bowie performed at the Freddie Mercury Tribute Concert, in April 1992, he was sufficiently moved by the occasion to drop to his knees and recite The Lord's Prayer.

Bono

The Eighties were responsible for many miracle makeovers, one of the most surprising being the transformation of U2 from third rate new wave band to stadium-fillers. Front-man Bono, who shared a Cleveland, Ohio stage with Bowie in 1990 for a version of Them's R&B classic 'Gloria', has since cleverly engineered a series of Bowie-like reinventions that enabled his band to successfully negotiate the ebb and flow of musical change during the Nineties.

John Lennon

They never shared a stage together, but Bowie's 1974 studio session with Lennon – one of only a handful of people who could inspire awe in Bowie – was his most fruitful all-star collaboration. After visiting the reclusive ex-Beatle at his Dakota apartment in New York (where producer Tony Visconti remembers Bowie being so nervous that he sat in a corner doodling), the pair collaborated on a version of Lennon's 'Across The Universe' and worked on a new song, 'Fame'. Not long afterwards Bowie admitted that John had also offered plenty of helpful advice concerning his business problems with Tony DeFries.

Marianne Faithfull

Bowie invited Marianne Faithfull to guest on *The 1980 Floor Show*, filmed for American TV at London's Marquee Club in October 1973. A potential rock'n'roll suicide who'd already survived one attempt to take her own life, Marianne was still obviously fragile. As the pair fumbled their way through Sonny & Cher's 1965 hit, 'I Got You Babe', her backless nun's costume prompted a few raised eyebrows from the backing musicians. According to Angie Bowie, David saw a whole lot more after the show. "He wanted to get in her pants. She'd been Mick's (*page 54*), so he had to have her as well."

Tina Turner

Bowie was regularly seen with the effervescent soul star during the Eighties, but mercifully their recorded output was restricted to just one song, the 1984 reggae-lite single 'Tonight'. The following year, he joined her on stage in Birmingham for a medley of two versions of 'Let's Dance' – Chris Montez's 1962 hit, and Bowie's 1983 original. They also duetted on a revamped 'Modern Love' for a Pepsi TV ad in 1987 (*below*).

Pet Shop Boys

If the album version of 1995's 'Hallo Spaceboy' was a pulverising piece of NIN-esque noise, then the single mix was an almost entirely re-recorded Eurodisco classic, featuring, at David's invitation, the acclaimed synth-pop duo. It became Bowie's biggest global hit of the Nineties, even going all the way to the top in Latvia.

Inside the grand Haddon Hall, 1970. Peter Noone's *Top Of The Pops* performance of 'Oh! You Pretty Things' in 1971, with David on piano, has been wiped by the BBC. Sadly, Bowie's stomp through 'The Jean Genie' the following year suffered the same fate.

Facing page: Long tresses and long dresses. "One day we will live next door to you and your lawn will die," was The Riot Squad's oft-repeated threat. But by April 1971, Bowie preferred to use his own back garden to model this Mr. Fish silk velour "man's dress". In 1999, ex-Dexy's singer, Kevin Rowland, pulled a similar stunt, with considerably less success.

1.5

The Man Who Bought The Dress

Between the mild-mannered faux-hippie pop star of 'Space Oddity' and the full-on androgyne of Ziggy Stardust, there was... that dress. Liz Hurley's little black number had nothing on Bowie's fetching Mr. Fish outfit – nothing apart from a few thousand acres of newsprint, that is.

For someone who thrived on symbols and change, the beginning of a new decade must have carried a near-spiritual significance. Tradition weighed "like a nightmare on the brains of the living", wrote 19th century longhair Karl Marx; now, as 1970 began, Bowie saw the new decade as an opportunity to level the playing-field. Somebody up there liked him, because weeks later, The Beatles split. Then The Rolling Stones announced they were emigrating. In an instant, pop's driving-seat was looking pretty vacant. Any takers for a man in a dress?

Bowie had proved himself with 'Space Oddity'. With a lucrative new publishing deal, secured by Tony DeFries, he began to feel like a real songwriter. With new guitarist, Mick Ronson, he had the right musical foil. And with Angie, whom he married in March 1970, and DeFries, he had all the emotional and business support he needed. It was an ambitious young crew with plenty of rock biz savvy. "We were all there for the purpose of making David Bowie a star," remembers producer Tony Visconti.

Bowie has always been fond of fish, even wearing two for this 1995 photo session. "The look was based on a piece by the Viennese artist, Rudolph Schwartzkogler," Bowie reveals.

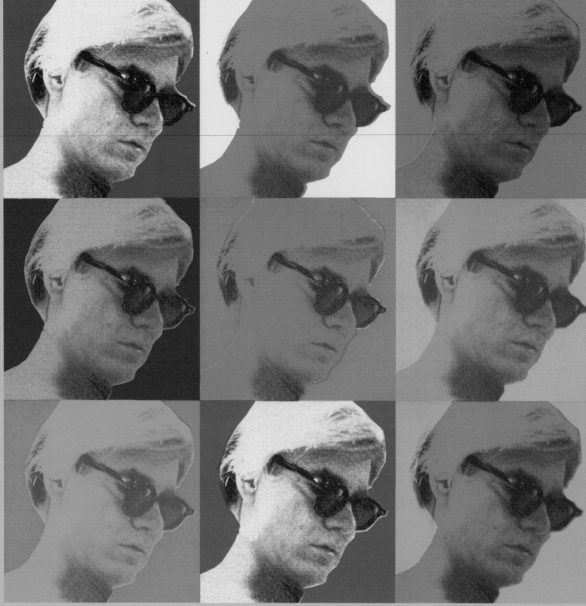

David Bowie has switched allegiances more times than even he probably cares to remember, but the single most enduring influence on his life and work, and the one that provides the key to his Seventies work, is pasty-faced Pop Art icon Andy Warhol. In 1973, at the height of Bowie's infatuation, he said: "I think that Warhol will… be regarded as just as important as Michaelangelo was to the art of his period." Time has not dimmed that view. In the mid-Nineties, at the opening of an exhibition of his own paintings, he repeated the claim: "Andy Warhol was one of the most influential and important

artists of the second half of this century. His ability was to confuse art enough that the boundaries started coming down so there was no division between high and low art."

Most Sixties and early Seventies rock musicians viewed themselves and their work through the prism of the literary Romantics, if at all. Idealists intoxicated on the pungent air of individual genius, they were maestros blessed with a peculiar gift. Despite being a gifted individual and a maestro of the peculiar, Andy Warhol subverted and shattered this rarefied world. OK, so blurring the boundaries

between commerce and fine art was hardly news to the gods of rock. But debunking the role of the 'artist' by depersonalising himself and getting others to do his work for him (in the studio he dubbed 'The Factory')? Why would he want to do that? Because, ultimately, nothing was truly original, or even particularly important; even humans were empty vessels at the mercy of what was being fed to them. "Why don't you tell me the words and I can just repeat them… I'm so empty that I can't think of anything," he told one interrogator. In presenting himself as artifice, as an

absent presence, as a charlatan and, perhaps, a master man-ipulator, Warhol became the most discussed artist of his generation.

Bowie first encountered Warhol's work via Ken Pitt, who met the artist in New York in November 1966 with a view to promoting his rock band protégés, The Velvet Underground, in Britain. Nothing came of the venture, but Pitt did return with an acetate of their first album, which he gave to David. A club-jazz version of 'Waiting For The Man', and a steal from 'Venus In Furs' in Bowie's 'Little Toy Soldier' (both recorded with The Riot Squad) soon followed.

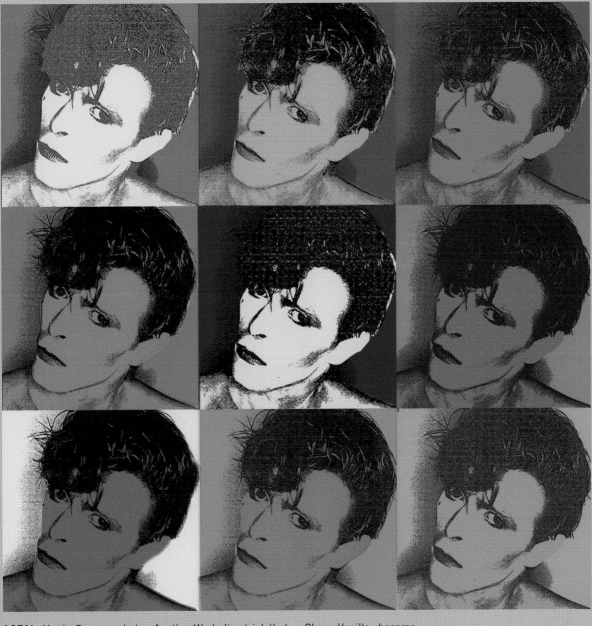

1971's *Hunky Dory* revealed the depth of Bowie's interest. 'Queen Bitch' was a brilliant take on VU-style street-sleaze; 'Andy Warhol' was an affectionate tribute to the artist that revealed Bowie's passion for Warholian artifice: "Dress my friends up just for show / See them as they really are". While in New York in 1971 on a promotional visit, he dropped in at the Factory and gave an impromptu performance of the song. Warhol obviously wasn't amused and walked out, only to return to utter a few kind words about Bowie's yellow Anello & Davide shoes as he photographed them.

Another Warholian trick that Bowie successfully aped was making himself the centre of a creative, circus-like whirl-wind. Projects like The Hype and Arnold Corns failed to get off the ground, partly because Bowie had yet to constitute any central point of focus, but between 1972 and 1973, he championed Mott The Hoople, Iggy Pop and Lou Reed with great success. Bowie and his new model army was the biggest self-help group since Brian Epstein floated his roster of Merseyside talents on the back of The Beatles. Even Bowie's entourage - which included Warhol acolytes Tony Zanetta and

Cherry Vanilla - became worthy of note.

Since Warhol's death in 1987, Bowie has paid tribute to him in song ("Andy, where's my 15 minutes?" on 'I Can't Read') and even portrayed Warhol on screen (*Basquiat, right*), his performance acclaimed by both Lou Reed and Warhol film director Paul Morrissey.

Showing off designer footwear, 1971. "These clothes were very London at the time. Everyone was wearing these camp little underground things. The shoes were canary yellow. And I expect the jacket is fuchsia. Like the enamel butterfly."

Trouser rehearsal for
The Man Who Sold
***The World* cover.**

Instead of capitalising on 'Space Oddity' with an identikit follow-up, Bowie's game-plan was to conduct musical warfare on several fronts. He began writing songs at the piano, in a manner not dissimilar to Paul McCartney, with a view to getting other stars to record them.

He adopted a pop Svengali role, surrounding himself with nonentities to whom he'd promise fame – or at least the opportunity to record one of his songs. He pursued his solo career with the enthusiasm of a newly liberated refugee: he tried his hand at hard rock (*The Man Who Sold The World*), Velvet Underground pastiches ('Queen Bitch') and singer-songwriter material ('Life On Mars?', 'Oh! You Pretty Things'). But first came the Hype, a maligned, misunderstood and ephemeral venture that anticipated both the ballsy playfulness and the sartorial intemperance of Glam Rock. David Bowie had decided to rock.

Hype: the very word was like a stentorian profanity in the vibey lingo of rockspeak. Hype was a curse on the scene, cheaply-purchased praise that masked a woeful lack of authenticity. "I suppose you could say that I chose Hype deliberately with tongue in cheek," Bowie said later. The quartet, which included Mick Ronson and Tony Visconti within its ranks, played its most infamous show in February 1970 at London's notorious hippie hang-out the Roundhouse. Each musician dressed in character. Bowie, in lurex tights, silver cape, scarves and pirate boots, was Rainbowman, flanked by Ronson's Gangsterman (in gold lame suit and fedora), Tony Visconti's Superman-inspired Hypeman and John Cambridge as Cowboyman. "Marc Bolan was the only person that clapped," Bowie subsequently claimed. But the event marked a watershed: "Theatre was for me after that". And bona fide rock music.

Fronting The Hype at the
Roundhouse,1970. The guitar
conceals Bowie's knickers over
his tights, Superman style:
"Very spacey, there was a lot of
lurex-y material in it. It was all
jeans and long hair at that time,
and we got booed all the way
through the show. It was great!"

Bowie's first rock album was *The Man Who Sold The World*. The cover, though, was pure theatre. He had come, he explained to *Rolling Stone*'s John Mendelsohn, "to tart rock up. I don't want to climb out of my fantasies in order to go up on stage – I want to take them on stage with me." But first he tried it out at Haddon Hall. He knew exactly what he wanted. As the photographer fiddled with his tripod, Bowie nestled his thin, languid frame into a chaise longue. His blond hair was long and peek-a-boo style like Veronica Lake's. More spectacular still, he was wearing what he described as his "man's dress". A salmon-pink silk number, it was one of two he'd bought from Mr. Fish at a knockdown £50 apiece, though in truth it was originally intended as a medieval-style gown.

The new image attracted the inevitable titters from the tabloids, but the hype-wary British rock press regarded Bowie's literal interpretation of unisex fashion as just plain silly. In America, where it was reported that he "would prefer to be regarded as a latter-day Garbo", and was "almost disconcertingly reminiscent of Lauren Bacall", they took him far more seriously. Perhaps the eye-shadow and shoulder-bag, which he'd added for his trip there, clinched it.

Bowie was now moving toward a different type of stardom, one that owed more to Andy Warhol's ironic and corrupted take on Hollywood than to the homilies of rock manners. "Pantomime Rock" it may well have been, but Bowie clearly understood the genuine need for a different kind of idol. Haughtily claiming that "Music is the Pierrot and I, the performer, am the message," he rejected rock's infatuation with technique and technology in favour of a personality-driven approach with one crucial difference – an all-knowing detachment.

In Bowie's hands, stardom wasn't merely a reward for artistic endeavour; it was inextricably part of the creative process, as crucial as chord changes and concert schedules. This was ingenious and revelatory. He wrote songs about Dylan and Warhol; he namedropped Lennon and Crowley.

He wasn't a star, but he was already learning to feed off their glamour.

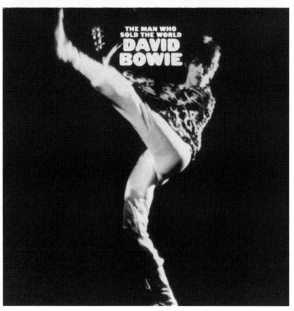

Above: Brian Ward's
equally potent cover for the
LP's re-release in 1972.

Far left: Lauren Bacall
and (*left*) Veronica Lake.

Facing page:
Sphinx, 1971. On the
threshold of becoming the
eighth wonder of the
world, Bowie inexplicably
adopts an Egyptian look.

Above: As the anarchic poet Herbert Beerbolm Baal for the BBC's *Play For Today*, screened in 1982.

Right: Bowie, Clark and Roeg on the set of *The Man Who Fell To Earth* in 1975.

In recent years, Bowie has played down his thespian pursuits: "The acting is purely decorative. It's not something I seriously entertain as an ambition." He didn't always see it that way. Back in the late Sixties, when he was having little luck as a singer, he attended auditions and accepted walk-on parts in TV plays – even an advert for ice-cream whenever he could. By 1973, having exhausted his Ziggy/ Aladdin role, he insisted that he'd tired of rock'n'roll and was entertaining a movie career. When it came, in the form of an alien in *The Man Who Fell To Earth*, director Nic Roeg told him, "Be yourself!"

Since then, Bowie has actively pursued a movie career, sometimes appearing in two of three films in a year. There have been one or two noteworthy performances – his portrayal of Major Jack Celliers, a Japanese prisoner-of-war, was convincing – but his finest and most taxing role was as John Merrick, the title part in the 1980 Broadway stage production of *The Elephant Man*. His involvement in too many unexceptional projects has no doubt sapped his enthusiasm for the medium; his only noteworthy role in recent years was playing Andy Warhol in *Basquiat*. But despite his professed lack of interest, he still makes more movies than albums.

As Thomas Jerome Newton in *The Man Who Fell To Earth*, Bowie passes up the offer to scrub Candy Clark's back. He's found something more interesting to look at.

Keeping his head, on the set of *Merry Christmas Mr Lawrence*, with director Nagisa Oshima (*above left*) in 1982. Bowie: "I've never had such an exhilarating experience working on a movie. I'd do a nudie film for him at the drop of a hat."

Facing page: As Prussian officer, Paul von Przygodsky in 1978's *Just A Gigolo.* "Listen, you were disappointed, and you weren't even in it. Imagine how we felt. It was my 32 Elvis Presley movies rolled into one."

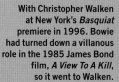

With Christopher Walken at New York's *Basquiat* premiere in 1996. Bowie had turned down a villanous role in the 1985 James Bond film, *A View To A Kill*, so it went to Walken.

During the Sixties, David Bowie moved with the fast-changing subcultural tide. He'd shown signs of rebellion during 1967, when he failed to be convinced by the Love Generation, but by the end of the decade he'd succumbed to the freak fraternity. The Seventies would be different. Buoyed by self-belief, and protected by a series of theatrical masks and Warhol-inspired strategies, he spent the decade reinventing himself according to his own whims and fancies, a one-man style warfare which altered the visual meaning – and impact – of rock and pop forever.

2.1 Ziggy Stardust

The creation of Ziggy Stardust was, wrote Bowie's ex-wife Angie in *Backstage Passes*, "the first emphatic act in a great liberation". The focal point was Bowie's 'cockade orange', the feather-cut from hell (or maybe Mars) that was conceived at Haddon Hall by Susie Fussey, a stylist from a local hairdresser's salon in Beckenham High Street, and held in place with a few generous squirts of a popular anti-dandruff treatment called Guard.

Angie described the Ziggy barnet as "the single most reverberant fashion statement of the Seventies" and for once her unquenchable thirst for exaggeration was justified. "He looked just as ambivalently enticing as he had with his long blond hippie hair," Angie maintained, "but this new, streamlined red puffball upped the ante. Now he looked stronger and wilder; just as fuckable, but a lot stranger and, well, more sluttish."

Designed by Freddi Burretti, David models a chocolate-brown suit with four-button double-breasted bum-freezer jacket, and 28-inch baggy trousers complete with two inches of turn-up, cut to be worn over platform boots.

Ziggy Stardust began life as a concept album about a character who descends from space to front what Bowie later described "feasibly the last band on earth". Because he'd been writing songs at an alarming rate, the idea inevitably became diluted by the time *The Rise And Fall Of Ziggy Stardust And The Spiders From Mars* was readied for release in June 1972. Nevertheless, the album provided a perfect springboard for Bowie to combine his quest for fame with his artistic needs. The results were hugely significant. Ziggy reopened lines to an alternative musical tradition (Velvet Underground, Iggy Pop); legitimised rock's ability to comment on itself (right down to the "Just who is Ziggy?" debate, prompted by RCA's famous "David Bowie Is Ziggy Stardust" campaign); took rock theatre into new dimensions; and blew open the related issues of gender and identity politics. Obviously, rock could never be the same again.

Years later, Bowie acknowledged that Ziggy's wardrobe – which he once described as "a cross between Nijinsky and Woolworth's" – had been a steal from Stanley Kubrick's *A Clockwork Orange*. "The jumpsuits in that I thought were just wonderful, and I liked the malicious, malevolent, vicious quality of those four guys, although aspects of violence themselves didn't turn me on particularly. I wanted to put another spin on that, so I... picked out all these very florid, bright, quilted kind of materials, and so that took the edge off the violent look of those suits, but still retained that terrorist, we're ready for action kind of look. And the wrestling boots... I changed the colour, made 'em greens and blues and things like that... It all fitted in perfectly with what I was trying to do, create this fake world, or this world that hadn't happened yet."

Lucky numbers. Ziggy plays guitar in Newcastle, January 1973. "Most people are scared of colour. Their lives are built up in shades of grey. It doesn't matter how straight the style is, make it brightly coloured material and everyone starts acting weird."

Facing page: Black shoes, white sox, October 1972. Bowie had seen the hairstyle in *Harpers & Queen*. "It was October 1971, the first report on the Japanese designer Kansai Yamamoto in England. He was using a Kabuki lion's wig on his models which was brilliant red. It was the most dynamic colour, so we tried to get mine as near as possible. I got Mick Ronson's ex-wife to cut my hair off short and dye it Schwarzkopf red. I got it to stand up with lots of blow-drying and this dreadful early lacquer."

Below: At BBC Television Centre's Studio 8, July 5, 1972: The *Top Of The Pops* performance of 'Starman' is without doubt the one key defining moment in post-Beatles rock history.

The one-hit wonderkid from 1969 was, by 1973, barely recognisable. Back then, people recognised his song but not the face. Now, with his lavatory-brush hair, pallid complexion, and risqué costumes revealing pole-like limbs, you couldn't miss him.

Prior to Glam Rock, rock musicians found the issue of stardom faintly embarrassing. Bowie, by building the concept into Ziggy Stardust, was able to join the new breed of 'Superstars' while simultaneously managing to transcend stardom's most sordid associations by merely 'playing' at the role. Bowie wasn't the first star of the Seventies because Marc Bolan got there first. Neither was he the most popular because Rod Stewart and Elton John sold more records than him. But he was by far the most intriguing, simply because he made stardom even more fantasy-inducing and ambiguous than it already was. As *Starlust*, Fred and Judy Vermorel's collection of fan-fantasies, confirms, David Bowie was the best aid to masturbation since the Kinsey Report.

Stardom, as John Lennon was fond of saying, was a form of madness. A decade's worth of Beatlemania left him nursing a fractured identity that prompted a retreat into primal therapy, and proclaiming that he didn't believe "in Beatles". Bowie fed off this debased take on stardom, also explored in the 1970 film *Performance*, starring Mick Jagger, claiming that he needed its distracting qualities: "Being famous helps put off the problems of discovering myself," he said.

Bowie was the baby-boomer who boomeranged a generation's hopes back into their faces. His Ziggy-style take on stardom was empty, fleeting and came gift-wrapped in a death-wish. It was Syd Barrett sacrificing himself to acid, turning his back on fame and taking the slow train to the psychiatric ward. It was Iggy Pop lacerating himself on stage. It was Vince Taylor announcing that he was Jesus Christ and being carted off to a rest home. It was Brian Jones and Jim Morrison getting fat and meeting watery ends. It was Jimi Hendrix choking on his own vomit. That was the kind of stardom into which David Bowie daringly dipped his gaily-painted toe.

When he wasn't telling friends he'd rather stay out of the sun in case he would melt, Bowie was enjoying the conventional trappings of stardom. He hung out with Mick Jagger, was on first-name terms with all the top maitre d's, and became a regular customer on the QE2. But a punishing work schedule of non-stop touring, with recording sessions, TV appearances and interviews fitted in whenever possible, inspired Bowie to construct Aladdin Sane, a son-of-Ziggy, based on his recent experiences. Replacing one mask with another enabled Bowie to exorcise what Ziggy had become – or so he thought. It wasn't enough. On July 3, 1973, in another melodramatic masterstroke, he announced his 'retirement' in front of an unsuspecting audience. He came to disarm stardom, but it would end up virtually destroying him.

Above, far left: Conversation Piece. Bowie performing 'Hang On To Yourself' on the Aladdin Sane tour in 1973.

Left: Sharing a joke about the fate of The Spiders with Lou Reed and Mick Jagger at the Cafe Royale 'retirement' party, July 3, 1973. Bowie had described Jagger as "incredibly sexy and very virile."

Strategically, Ziggy was a masterstroke. If Bowie was too coy to take a protean leap from the underground into pop's mainstream, as his rival Marc Bolan had done, why not get someone else to do it for him. That's the idea that began to form in Bowie's mind during 1971 and the early months of 1972, as rock'n'roll revivalism in the star-shaped form of Glam Rock emerged to fill the void left by The Beatles. Rejoicing in this new spirit of playfulness and musical economy were big personalities with oodles of well-honed talent – Elton John, Rod Stewart and Gary Glitter had, like Bowie and Bolan, been on the margins for years. Outsmarting them all, Bowie – as Ziggy – emerged during the summer of 1972 amid a rash of contradictions. Rock or pop? Gay or straight? Freak or fraud? Saviour or destroyer? No one knew for sure, but they couldn't stop talking about him.

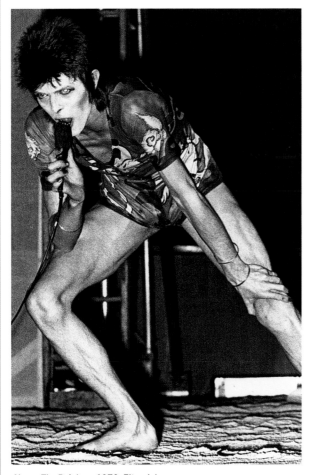

Above: The Rainbow, 1972. Elton John: "I've been following him since 'Space Oddity'. And I've followed him from all those albums that didn't sell, like *The Man Who Sold The World* and things like that. Above all, apart from all the glamorous rubbish, the music's there. *Ziggy Stardust* is a classic album."

When the Ziggy Stardust tour was officially launched – with little fanfare – at the Toby Jug in Tolworth, Surrey, in February 1972, David Bowie was simply promoting his latest album, *Hunky Dory*, and previewing songs from his forthcoming record. By the time his virtual non-stop concert schedule reached the Royal Festival Hall, London, in July, to mark Ziggy's release, he greeted his audience with the words: "Hello, I'm Ziggy Stardust and these are The Spiders From Mars".

As Bowie and his Ziggy doppelganger reaped greater success, the aloofness that critic Ray Coleman had picked up on at the Festival Hall, had intensified. The shows became more theatrical, with a dance troupe, images projected onto the stage, moveable scaffolding, even the piped sound of Beethoven's Ninth Symphony, lifted from the soundtrack of *A Clockwork Orange*. "A Bowie concert is your old Busby Berkeley production... this was perhaps the most consciously theatrical rock show ever staged," wrote Charles Shaar Murray, not entirely positively. David Bowie had become the Star of '72, but there was already distinct unease with what he was up to.

"I surrounded myself with people who indulged my ego. They treated me as though I was Ziggy Stardust or one of my characters, never realising that David Jones might be behind it."

There was similar disquiet on a personal level. Asked in 1974 whether he believed Ziggy was "a monster", Bowie replied, "Oh, he certainly was... When I first wrote it was just an experiment. It was an exercise for me and he really grew sort of out of proportion, I suppose, got much bigger than I thought Ziggy was going to be... Ziggy just overshadowed everything." Years later, Bowie admitted that Ziggy prompted "real problems, because I enjoyed the character so much and it was so much easier for me to live within that character that, along with the help of some chemical substances at the time, it became easier and easier for me to blur the lines between reality and the blessed creature that I'd created, my doppelganger... The doppelganger and myself were starting to become one and the same person. And then you start on this trail of chaotic psychological destruction."

Knowingly passing himself off as another character, and announcing that artifice was at the heart of his game, wasn't merely a triumph of rock aesthetics; it was crucial to Bowie's career. Angie Bowie: "It's somewhat trite, but it's true: by creating Ziggy to go out and front for him, David never had to act like himself in public if he didn't want to, which in turn meant that he could pursue art and applause without having to deal with his lack of self-esteem, as the shrinks put it, or more accurately, his frigid self-loathing."

"There was one time when I saw him being made up for a Russell Harty show, and I remember looking at his reflection in the mirror and thinking, 'This is the most beautiful man I've ever seen'. I don't remember him being camp at any time but he was beautiful. It comes from the bone structure I think. It was *beauty* as opposed to handsomeness." - Ziggy producer, Ken Scott.

THE ZIGGY ENIGMA

Bowie's most enigmatic creation, who rose from anonymity to revered idol status only to throw it all away, was a dashing exercise of wish-fulfilment that said much about his own aspirations and thirst for melodrama. Bowie-as-Ziggy soon mutated into pop's most pampered laboratory animal, but he could never have made it without a little help from his friends...

Iggy Pop

Prefix Iggy's name with the oddest letter in the alphabet. Simple, wasn't it? (Bowie has since claimed, unconvincingly, that 'Ziggys' was the name of a tailor's shop he glimpsed from a train). According to the MainMan Vice-President Leee Black Childers, Bowie was infatuated with Iggy because he "wanted to tap into the rock'n'roll reality that Iggy lived – and that David Bowie could never live because he was a wimpy little South London art student and Iggy was a Detroit trash bag". Bowie returned the favour by overseeing three classic Iggy albums, *Raw Power* (1973), *The Idiot* and *Lust For Life* (both 1977). The pair, who were virtually inseparable during 1976 and 1977, have worked together intermittently ever since.

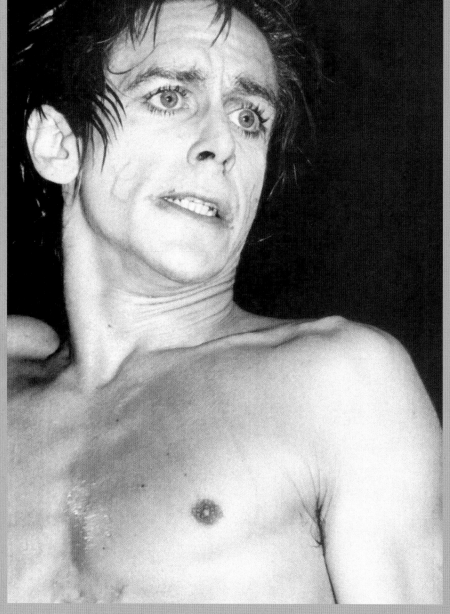

Vince Taylor

"Vince Taylor really became one of the building blocks of the Ziggy character. I just thought he was too good to be true; he was of another world, he was something else, and he was definitely part of the blueprint of thus strange character that came from somewhere." During the Nineties, Bowie has been keen to stress the importance of this little-known rock'n'roller to his Ziggy project.

Taylor, alias plain Brian Holden from California via Middlesex, found few takers for his second-wave rock'n'roll in London, so he fled to France where he was hailed as the new Elvis. Bowie met him in London in 1966, by which time Taylor was, Bowie recalled, "right out of his tree; this guy was bonkers, absolutely the genuine article. I can't remember if he said he was an alien or the Son of God, but he might have been a bit of both."

Taylor returned to France, but a 1967 tour ended in catastrophe. "At his last performance," Bowie told Paul Du Noyer, "he dismissed the band, then went on stage dressed in white robes as Jesus Christ and said, 'I am the Resurrection, I am Jesus Christ.' They nearly lynched him." A bona fide leper Messiah, indeed. Vince Taylor died in Switzerland in 1991.

There was little contact between Glam rivals Bowie and Bolan (*left*) during the Ziggy period. However, a few years back David revealed that he is in possession of tapes featuring some top-secret demo recordings he made with Marc in Los Angeles in the mid-Seventies.

play guitar". There were just too many obvious references in the title track (let's put "snow-white tan" down to artistic licence) for Ziggy to have been anyone else.

Other theories…

The Nazz, Todd Rundgren's band.

Both Alice Cooper and Todd Rundgren fronted Sixties bands called The Nazz, which again could be a reference to the Nazarin, alias Jesus Christ… Before he turned his back on stardom claiming he'd seen the light after a particularly potent acid trip, Fleetwood Mac's Peter Green had taken to wearing robes like the man from Galilee or, perhaps, a "leper Messiah". Another counterculture idol with the whiff of Rise and Fall about him was longtime Bowie favourite Pink Floyd's Syd Barrett. The potentially tragic nature of pop stardom was the subject of a cult movie, *Privilege*, starring Sixties heart-throb Paul Jones and released in 1967. That same year, pop mythologist Nik Cohn published *I Am Still The Greatest Says Johnny Angelo*, a fictional tale concerning the rise and fall of a pulp hero. "Violence and glamour and speed, splendour and vulgarity, danger and gesture and style – these were the things that he valued, nothing else." And, yes, Bowie read the book… Whether he saw the cult voyeur movie *Peeping Tom* is not known, but the similarity between the very first scene and the cover of the *Ziggy Stardust* album is uncanny.

Marc Bolan
Bowie was at once fascinated and consumed with envy when his pal and rival Marc Bolan made a virtually overnight transformation from hippie throwback to the first idol of Glam Rock. Bolan, who spouted poetry, wore make-up and sported Medusa-like hair, was a strange kind of pop star; cue Ziggy Stardust, the ultimate rock'n'roll oddity. Bolan's influence didn't stop there. Ziggy acolytes "Weird and Gilly" sound like characters plucked from an old Bolan poem. And suspicions that the T Rex man inspired 'Lady Stardust' were confirmed when his face was projected onto a screen during a performance of the song at the Rainbow in August 1972.

The Legendary Stardust Cowboy
One evening, a little-known country and western singer was invited on to the popular American comedy show, *Rowan & Martin's Laugh-In*. The audience thought him hilarious; the singer, the self-styled Legendary Stardust Cowboy, wasn't so amused and reportedly fled the stage in tears. His music was, Bowie fondly recalled, "the most anarchic, nihilistic stuff you've ever heard in your life", and as early as 1972 he was openly acknowledging Ziggy's debt to the Legendary One.

Jimi Hendrix
Jimi "played it left-hand", was infamously "well-hung" and, when he wore his Oriental headscarf, sported a "screwed-down hairdo / Like some cat from Japan". Hendrix was rock's gifted, if reluctant superstar whose three years of fame and narcotic obliteration came to an abrupt end in September 1970. He was "loaded", certainly, but "boy could he

2.2

Aladdin Sane

My Death: "I saw him do it in '73. I was so impressionable then that he could have done a Rolf Harris song and I'd have thought it was mega." - Echo And The Bunnymen's Ian McCulloch.

Ziggy Stardust had been Bowie's Glam Rock space cadet infused with an impudent dash of *A Clockwork Orange*. Aladdin Sane was Ziggy writ larger, and even more incomprehensible. The key motif was a lightning flash uncannily similar to the international symbol for danger. Everything that Ziggy threatened to become manifested itself in Aladdin Sane. It was a creation that very nearly overwhelmed its creator.

Bowie later described Aladdin Sane as "Ziggy goes to America. I'd said all I could say about Ziggy but I created this bloody thing, now how do I get out of it." America was, in Bowie's eyes, "this alternative world that I'd been talking about. It had all the violence and all the strangeness and the bizarreness and it was really happening. It was like real life. It wasn't just in my songs." Unlike Ziggy, which had been created in Bowie's imagination, Aladdin Sane was about the reality of stardom.

The studious, Warhol-like detachment which Bowie had applied to Ziggy Stardust barely got a look-in during the Aladdin Sane era, which seemed to take hold during the three-month US tour towards the end of 1972. When Bowie made a fleeting national appearance on the *Russell Harty Plus* TV show, early in 1973, it was as if the "leper Messiah" had finally landed. The singer who, not 18 months earlier, had disappointed several of Andy Warhol's friends for resembling a "folky old hippie" now epitomised everything that ran counter to popular, and even unpopular, taste. "My next role will be a person called Aladdin Sane," he said. No one was in any doubt that he was already playing the part.

In many ways, this was Bowie's most perfect creation – the moment when Frankenstein's monster finally walked. But the parallels with the visionary scientist were all too clear: at 110 lbs, Bowie was painfully thin and corpse-like, and wore the look of someone in the grip of forces that were about to destroy him. One of the songs he performed on the show was Jacques Brel's 'My Death'; it sounded like a funeral dirge. His favourite reading at the time was Robert Heinlein's *Stranger In A Strange Land*.

The *Aladdin Sane* lightning bolt was Bowie's most recognisable insignia in the Seventies. "I came up with the flash thing. But the teardop was (photographer) Brian Duffy's. He put that on afterward. I thought it was rather sweet." Twenty years later, when Bowie saw what Jones Bloom had painted on to this Q cover, he described it as "cheeky".

Facing page: 'Drive In Saturday' was also performed on the same TV show. The song, Bowie recalls, had been "written for Mott The Hoople. But they decided the time had come for them to write their own single, so it was given back to me. I was so annoyed, that one night in Florida I got very drunk and shaved my eyebrows off!"

Kim Novak celebrated her 45th birthday with co-star Bowie on the set of *Just A Gigolo* in February 1978.

The 'Miracle Goodnight' video-shoot, Los Angeles, February 1993.

Rumours of David Bowie's bisexuality did wonders for his heterosexual health. "I've had all these girls try to get me over to the other side again, 'C'mon, David, it isn't all that bad, I'll show you'," he said later. Sex was never just a gimmick for Bowie. His work is littered with innuendo and graphic sexual references, and his narcissistic and voyeuristic tendencies are well documented. After discovering sex at 14, he recalled that, "My first thought was, well, if I ever get sent to prison, I'll know how to keep happy."

For many years, particularly during the Seventies, Bowie consumed groupies with the enthusiasm of a Viagra-chomping rabbit. But a keen appetite for carnal pleasures hasn't prevented him from enjoying – and in one or two cases enduring – several meaningful, long-term relationships.

In 1976, when Bowie was probably at his most cynical, he was asked about love. "Never have been in love, to speak of. I was in love once, maybe, and it was an awful experience. It rotted me, drained me, and it was a disease… Being in love is something that breeds brute anger and jealousy, every-thing but love, it seems." His comments suggested a deep psychological need to protect himself from emotional pain – rejecting 'love' offered the same kind of protection that Warholian strategies con-ferred on his public life.

The object of Bowie's invective was Hermione Farthingale: tall, beautiful, artistic and a classic English rose of middle class stock (and with a name to die for). The pair met late in 1967 while both attended Lindsay Kemp's mime and dance classes. They appeared briefly together for a scene in a BBC-TV drama, *The Pistol Shot*, and by spring 1968 had fallen in love. In August, Bowie moved out of Ken Pitt's central London flat to share an attic bedsit with Hermione in Kensington.

Temporarily ditching plans for a solo career, he formed Feathers, a folksy, mixed-media trio with Hermione, who danced, sang occasion-ally and provided a fine foil for Bowie and the guitar-playing John Hutchinson. The threesome appeared in *Love You Till Tuesday*, a 30-minute promotional film shot early in 1969. But days after it was completed, Hermione ended the relationship, apparently at the behest of her parents, who thought she deserved better than a struggling pop singer.

Ken Pitt remembers Bowie returning to his flat "bruised and insecure". Deeply traumatised might have been more accurate, for years later, Bowie was still affected by the loss: "We had a perfect love, so perfect that it burned out in two years. We were too close, thought alike and spent all the time in a room sitting on the corner of the bed." The last phrase reprised a line from 'An Occasional Dream', one of two songs on Bowie's 1969 album which dealt with the episode. 'Letter To Hermione' was more revealing: "I tear my soul to ease the pain," sang Bowie, but by 1970, hurt had turned to bitterness: "She took my head / Smashed it up / Left my young blood rising," so "I grabbed her golden hair / And threw her to the ground." The title, 'She Shook Me Cold', said it all. Some insist that Hermione has reappeared as "the girl with the mousey hair" in 'Life On Mars?', or even as Ziggy Stardust. More certain is that Bowie never allowed himself to give so much to another partner, at least not for many years.

At London's Cafe Royale for a *Just A Gigolo* press call, with co-star Sydne Rome, Valentine's Day 1979.

Clowning about at the Alacazar Club in Paris with Coco Schwab, May 1976.

Bowie wrote 'Even A Fool Learns To Love' when he was with Hermione Farthingale. Ken Pitt: "She was very much a muse. A delightful girl, and the complete antithesis of Angie, but I don't think they were at all matched. I was later told that she left after another man reappeared in her life."

1969's 'The Wild Eyed Boy From Freecloud' was apparently written for Mary Finnegan's son, Richard.

With his good looks and lively mind, Bowie has had no shortage of women admirers, including more than his fair share of posh girls seeking a bit of rock'n'roll excitement. An early encounter with wealth and taste came via Dana Gillespie, a 14-year-old drama student with a passion for gorgeous and creative R&B singers. Already well on the way to achieving her famous 44-26-37 figure, Dana picked out her favourite Manish Boy one 1964 evening at the Marquee Club and smuggled him home for a night of passion. The pair quickly became soul-mates, meeting at coffee-houses and, later, in Dana's own flat, though

with her eyes on Bob Dylan and his on making it, the relationship cooled. Dana remained a long-term fixture in Bowie's life, helping him to pick up the pieces after Hermione's departure and again during the mid-Seventies, when he was going through a particularly traumatic spell.

Between Dana and Hermione came Natasha Kornilof, a costume and set designer who was Lindsay Kemp's chief competitor for Bowie's affections during the winter of 1967-68. The affair was conducted between bouts of painting scenery backdrops, but petered out after Kemp "scratched" his wrists and she downed too

many sleeping pills one night. Kornilof later designed Bowie's costumes for his 1978 world tour but her most memorable creation was the 1980 Pierrot outfit for 'Ashes To Ashes'.

After a brief fling with journalist Mary Finnigan, who gave Bowie a spare room in her Beckenham flat, listened eagerly to his thoughts on Buddhism, and helped him set up the Beckenham Arts Lab, Bowie found his perfect mate – a 19-year-old business studies student and American motormouth Mary Angela Barnett. She nursed and cultivated his ego, demanding little more than the opportunity to parade her star-in-waiting like a prize kitten. Angie's support was crucial: she hassled record companies, agents and journalists; encouraged her shy English boy to get out a bit and mingle with the rock crowd; and provided the magic ring of confidence he needed.

The couple met on 9 April 1969; within a year, they'd married. Some whispered it was merely a ruse so that David could obtain the Green Card that would enable him to live and work in America. Not that there was much chance of that happening when the pair stepped out of Bromley Registry Office on 20 March 1970 as man and wife. Bowie was struggling to capitalise on the success of 'Space Oddity', was in the process of ditching his manager and showed little inclination to perform live or even to write new material.

With Bianca Jagger leaving Paris nightspot Chez Castel, June 1977.

By 1973, all that had changed. Dave'n'Angie had become a mutant version of those old-school sophisticates Mick'n'Bianca, guaranteed to create headlines wherever they went, but both had already outlived each other's usefulness. Monogamy had never been central to their relationship, but now living in Chelsea, in the heart of rock star territory, the favours came thicker and faster. While Angie was out on huge shopping sprees, or trying to get her modelling career off the ground, David entertained a stream of women in their exclusive residence in Oakley Street. When one, a startling black teenager from Chicago named Ava Cherry, moved in (initially at Angie's request), the strain was too much and Ava was packed off to a nearby flat.

Bowie originally wrote *Hunky Dory*'s 'Andy Warhol' for Dana Gillespie to sing.

Backstage at Rona Barrett's *Good Morning America* TV show with Angie, 1975

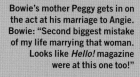

Bowie's mother Peggy gets in on the act at his marriage to Angie. Bowie: "Second biggest mistake of my life marrying that woman. Looks like *Hello!* magazine were at this one too!"

Facing page: With Iman at LAX Airport, Los Angeles, 1992.

Ava Cherry, the funk-soul sister.

Love Is Strange. With Romy Haag at the Alcazar Club in Paris, May 1976.

Social Kind Of Girl. Partying with Susan Sarandon in New York, 1983.

With Melissa Hurley in 1989. She'd been a dancer on Bowie's Glass Spider tour.

While Angie became increasingly irrelevant, Ava was fresh, fun – and different. "He was fascinated by black people," she told the Gillmans. "Black girls, any girls he would sleep with when I was with him were black." That's when he wasn't enjoying brief liaisons with Salvador Dali's muse Amanda Lear, Marianne Faithfull or, later in the decade, Berlin tranny Romy Haag. Bowie found further exotic thrills in the company of two older women, Oona

Chaplin and Elizabeth Taylor, but by the mid-Seventies, the dominant woman in his life was his assistant 'Coco'. MainMan's gloriously shambolic organisational structure gave Coco, alias Corrine Schwab, a former assistant to UK concert promoter Peter Bowyer, the opportunity to rise from secretary in the London office to David's personal assistant during the '74 US tour. Stepping into the vacuum created by the stand-off between Bowie and Tony DeFries, her composure and cultured manner was exactly what Bowie needed during this strained period of his life. But her ascent to the top, which was complete by the late Seventies, won her enemies. Some insisted the iron curtain she wrapped around her charge was a way of disarming rivals. Others suggested that Coco was another Bowie creation, a surrogate mother who did his dirty work for him – and took the flak for it, so that David's genial reputation remained untarnished. Rumours that the pair were to marry were rife during the mid-Eighties, but unfounded; Coco remains Bowie's loyal and trusted advisor.

Dalliances with Jee Ling, the Chinese actress who enjoyed a tender moment with Bowie during the 'China Girl' video, Marie Helvin,

Susan Sarandon and Latin dancer Melissa Hurley (who was engaged to Bowie for over two years) during the Eighties seemed inconsequential by comparison.

Bowie looked destined to live his days out as a playboy divorcee until one night in October 1990, when he was introduced to a 34-year-old Somalian model, Iman Abdul Majid, at a Los Angeles dinner party arranged by his hairdresser Teddy Antolin.

It was, he said later, love at first sight. Independent, beautiful, financially secure and "not the usual sort of bubblehead that I'd known in the past". Iman aroused Bowie's dormant desire for genuine romantic involvement, and he wooed her with cruises in the Adriatic and trips to Japan, where they cemented their relationship with his'n'hers tattoos. On their first anniversary David proposed on the banks of the river Seine, backed up by "the Sinatra thing" 'April In Paris'. The couple were

married in a civil ceremony in Switzerland in April 1992, and repeated the event for the benefit of their friends and *Hello!* magazine in Florence, Italy, in June. Bowie, dressed in a suit he co-designed with Thierry Mugler, wrote the incidental music. He now claims to be a changed man: "There was a time when I couldn't look at a woman without evaluating her on a sexual basis. It's wonderful that it doesn't happen anymore. Turning 50 helped. My libido has started shrinking!" So far, so good.

With Iman at London's Cork Street, 1995. Their first child together is due in August 2000.

With Coco Schwab in the Royal Box at Live Aid, 1985.

Not sure if you're a boy or a girl. Amanda Lear's escorts during the Seventies numbered several well known rock stars

No outfit was out of bounds to Bowie, even maternity wear. "Nobody understood the European way of dressing and adopting the asexual, androgynous everyman pose. People all went screaming, "He's got make-up on and he's wearing stuff that looks like dresses."

Bowie finally met Kansai Yamamoto when he toured Japan in April 1973. "He presented me with virtually an entire wardrobe because he knew I was wearing copies of his stuff and he realised Ziggy was becoming very popular. It was the first real connection between a designer and a rock star."

By this time, The Sweet, Gary Glitter, Rod Stewart and even The Rolling Stones had discovered the joys of dressing-up, but Bowie's rapid-fire make-overs left them all standing. It wasn't unusual for him to make up to six costume changes a night during the first half of 1973. Now heavily influenced by the dramatic make-up, role-play and costumes of Japanese Kabuki theatre, he'd commissioned a complete new wardrobe from the Japanese designer Kansai Yamamoto, the centre-piece being his magnificent 'Spring Rain' costume, which he whipped off to reveal a range of under-garments that included a sumo wrestler's truss, blue-and-red striped leotards and micro-bikinis. His hair, now almost unnaturally angular, had grown longer and was set off by a round, Pierre Laroche-designed reflector on his forehead. (Laroche also styled the *Aladdin Sane* LP cover.)

"This was the first Japanese costume that I got. Originally worn by a woodland creature, that's why it has funny little animals on it."

Facing page: In 1999, David was asked if he could recall what the writing on the Japanese cloak said. His reply? "It may well have said, 'Get your potatoes here'."

TOBACCO SERIOUSLY DAMAGES HEALTH

Bowie has managed to kick cocaine, booze binges and groupies. He's even had his notoriously crooked teeth fixed. But despite dipping into Allen Carr's *The Easy Way To Stop Smoking*, listening to self-help tapes, acupuncture and hypnotherapy, his love/hate relationship with cigarettes continues unabated. "Filling your mouth with cement helps immeasurably," is his most recent, resigned statement on the likelihood of him packing it in.

Like many of his generation, Bowie associated the cigarette with Hollywood glamour (Dietrich, Bogart, Sinatra, *right and below*), intellectual freedom (Sartre, Kerouac), and bad boys (the spiv). The fact that his father smoked heavily failed to diminish its stylish appeal. "I was still very gawky and awkward and wanting to find my attitude. Cigarettes sort of supplied it quite easily."

Bowie switched brands during the early Eighties. "I can't think of a time that I didn't think about death," he told Pulp frontman, Jarvis Cocker but by swapping the strong taste of Gitanes for medium-strength Marlboro reds, he was making a mild concession to health concerns. By 1988, he'd switched again, to Marlboro Lights.

Starting with the occasional Weights cigarette nicked from his dad, the thrill-seeking David Jones soon graduated to Dominos, purchased in twos from a local newsagent. While working for an advertising agency in central London, he followed the example of several illustrators there and began to experiment with a variety of exotic, invariably foreign brands. Settling on Gitanes, a pungent and strong French smoke, he soon acquired a hefty habit that, during its mid-Seventies peak, saw him get through up to four packets per day. Fags found their way into his songs ("Time takes a cigarette / Puts it in your mouth"), became a vital accessory in publicity shots, a theatrical device on stage (he always used a match to light up) and an integral part of his iconography.

FILTER CIGARETTES

Marlboro

TOBACCO SERIOUSLY DAMAGES HEALTH

"You can tell with one drag . . . You're smoking smooth—smoking clean!"

Chesterfield presents Frank Sinatra. ABC-TV Friday nights— Live Première October 18 Full Hour

Chesterfield
CIGARETTES

CHESTERFIELD
KING and REGULAR

Proof that fags weren't good for David's health came in November 1991 when a pack of Marlboro tossed on stage by a female fan at the Brixton Academy caught him in the eye. Nevertheless, he gamely puffs on: today, Bowie enjoys his first cigarette of the day with a coffee after breakfast, and hits the pillow each night with the satisfaction of having devoured another 39 or so during the course of the day.

Ciggy and Iggy: the only time they ever shared the vocals on stage, New York's China Club, December 1985.

CIGGY POP

Expectations for the *Aladdin Sane* album, issued in April 1973, proved impossible to live up to. Bowie was the most talked-about rock star in the world, but the record was mildly denounced as hurried and inconsistent – exactly the qualities that have since made it more durable than its predecessor. Interspersed between the raids on vintage rock'n' roll ('The Jean Genie', 'Panic In Detroit', a version of the Rolling Stones' 'Let's Spend The Night Together') were nods to the German theatre song tradition ('Time'), the avant-garde ('Aladdin Sane') and galvanised New York rock ('Cracked Actor').

At a show in New York in February 1973, Bowie made his entrance via a descending cage lit by a single spotlight and with revolving mirrored globes on either side. What followed was a typically controlled performance with Bowie returning in six-inch heels for a finale of 'Rock'n'Roll Suicide'. But he hadn't reckoned on a fan leaping onto the stage and planting a kiss on his cheek. Bowie fainted, fell to the ground and was hastily carried off, leaving the audience wondering whether it had just witnessed the death of Ziggy Stardust/Aladdin Sane. Or even David Bowie.

Whoever he was, he lived on, at least until that night in July 1973 when Bowie retired Ziggy/Aladdin and quite possibly himself. Ulterior motives lurked behind the 'instant' decision to quit as Bowie later admitted: "I knew it was the end of the Spiders. I knew that I'd done as much as I could in the context of that band." Days after the show, he justified his decision: "That's what Ziggy did and so I had to do it too... I was in that particular frame of mind, that I was Ziggy and this had to be done. I had to finish the band... Vince Taylor had done the same thing. He just stopped and then they carted him away. It was part of a pattern, a self-fulfilling prophesy." Retirement didn't necessarily mean being "carted away": in 1965, after his Flowers exhibition in Paris, Andy Warhol announced his retirement from painting to concentrate on films – and never looked back.

Performing 'Love Me Do' with guest guitarist Jeff Beck at London's Hammersmith Odeon, July 3, 1973.

Watch That Man. At New York's Radio City Music Hall, Valentine's Day 1973.

Left: Bowie wore this Freddi Burretti-designed suit, the jacket of intricately patterned worsted, with ruby velvet trim and cream lining, on the *Russell Harty Plus* show in January 1973. It was sold at Christie's auctioneers in 1998 for £2,600.

Facing page: No less than three packs of Marlboros in evidence, at a Lulu playback at the Château d'Herouvillé, near Paris, July 1973.

Following pages: London, May 1973, backstage at Peter Cook and Dudley Moore's *Behind The Fridge*. Bowie was accompanied by Tony Visconti, the first time they'd seen each other in three years: "The David that I knew had mousy brown hair, and he walks into the kitchen with spiky orange hair, no eyebrows and a metallic suit. Our nanny dropped my son's bottle on the floor when she saw him!" The 'Life On Mars?' video shoot.

For the first half of his career, David Bowie regarded business matters as something that other people did. As a teenage hopeful, he was too busy waiting for his picture to appear in the papers to read the small print in his contracts. Besides, as he wasn't earning much, 50% of nothing hardly mattered.

When the cash began to roll in during the early Seventies, Bowie was living the life of a pampered superstar and profligacy prevailed. One day, late in 1974, he woke up in his hotel room and realised the party he'd been subsidising for the past three years was over. But the hangover, in terms of legal battles and financial follies, had several years yet to run. In the midst of his 1976 Station To Station tour, he announced to *Melody Maker's* Chris Charlesworth that he was broke, an exaggeration perhaps but then David was never one to let the whole truth get in the way of a spectacular quote.

Chicago, October 1972. Tony Defries once said of Bowie: "He always looks like a refugee unless he's been properly dressed and put together for the day."

By the early Eighties, Bowie had extricated himself from most of his obligations to MainMan and began to invest in art and antiques. In 1997 he raised further capital by selling the sound and publishing rights to his catalogue via a bond scheme. This enabled him to buy out DeFries completely; Bowie now controls his master-tapes outright. He has houses in several corners of the world and a wife with her own bank account. David Bowie won't get fooled again.

Bowie's first proper manager was Leslie Conn, an associate of Dick James who spectacularly failed to interest The Beatles' publisher in either Marc Feld (later Bolan) or David Jones. But he did manage to get David a deal with Decca/Vocalion, a spot on *Juke Box Jury*, and help fabricate the great hair debate. But after Parlophone delayed the release of Davy Jones and the Lower Third's 'You've Got A Habit Of Leaving' in 1965, the partnership was amicably dissolved.

A man of wealth and taste. "I do tend to regard money as the oil to get other things going. I feel more comfortable with it like that."

The King Of Stamford Hill: Les Conn was seen at the launch of Bowie's Cork Street art show, at the artist's special invitation.

"To be a star, you must act like one, regardless of expense," declared Tony DeFries. "DeFries was a disaster. He managed *himself* very well," adds his predecessor Ken Pitt.

A fine talker, DeFries was a firm believer in the Col. Tom Parker school of pop management: butter up the client, always brandish a big cigar and don't pull any punches. He promised David Bowie everything he wanted – fame, money and complete artistic control. As good as his word, he quickly secured a £5,000 publishing deal, which instantly unlocked Bowie's flagging creativity. Ignoring the pleas of David's record company, DeFries took him off to New York where he inked a lucrative new deal with RCA Records. Within a year, he'd tied up the master-tapes of Bowie's music with his company, MainMan, and had begun to liken himself to MGM movie magnate Louis B. Mayer.

Next came Ralph Horton, who chauffeured Bowie to shows in a Jaguar, gave him a place to stay and recommended various image changes. Within a year, the baillifs came knocking and Horton lost David to a publicist friend who recommend that the singer make a go of it as a soloist. He was Ken Pitt, a key influence in Bowie's life who invited his protégé to share his split-level bachelor-pad and nurtured a cultural revolution. (Bowie later described his stay chez Pitt as "one of the most stimulating periods of my life".)

The arrival of Angie, and then Tony DeFries, both of whom were more attuned to the increasingly hard-nosed rock industry, signalled Pitt's downfall, which ended messily after a showdown in May 1970. ("Ken is a very nice man," Bowie said later, "but that's not enough in this business.") DeFries was one of a new breed of legal trainees who eschewed formal qualifications in favour of busking it in the lucrative rock and pop market.

Like all empires, MainMan cracked under the weight of its own success. If excess and decadence was the nature of Bowie's game, MainMan more than did its best to match it. By late 1974, with a queue of debtors at the door, DeFries embarked upon his final, magnificent folly – *Fame*, a Broadway stage musical loosely based on the life of Marilyn Monroe. It lasted one night and lost £250,000. It was the final straw for Bowie, who struck a secret deal with his record company and then began the lengthy process of disengaging himself from MainMan. The settlement was painful: David was compelled to split the earnings of his early Seventies records in perpetuity and, even more galling, MainMan was entitled to a 16% share of Bowie's gross earnings until

September 1982. It was a huge sacrifice, but he had little alternative.

Bowie's attempt to exercise greater vigilance over his business affairs foundered barely a year into his partnership with Michael Lippman, who'd engineered the split from DeFries. Los Angeles lawyer Stanley Diamond helped him pick up the pieces, advising him to move to Switzerland, and lay some secure financial foundations. Bowie, too, began to dabble in fiscal

matters, and by the early Eighties he had set up several companies and helped negotiate a lucrative five-album deal with EMI. He'd settled with his ex-wife Angie and now stipulated loyalty clauses when recruiting new musicians. By the mid-Eighties, Bowie was probably worth £30 million; his two world tours during the decade earned him another £50 million or so. Current estimates put his wealth into the £200 million-plus bracket.

Talking 'bout Monroe at London's National Portrait Gallery, March 1995. "I'm managing myself now simply because I've got fed up with the managers I've known."

"I still recieve a special Christmas gift from David every year," says Ken Pitt.

It's Only Rock 'n' Roll. "An outfit is an entire life experience. An outfit is much more than just something to wear. It's about who you are, it's a badge and it becomes a symbol."

2.3

Soul Survivor

It would have been impossible for David Bowie to have surpassed the Zeitgeist-defining impact of his Ziggy Stardust and Aladdin Sane creations, but as he proved with his next moves, he hadn't lost the ability to shock. Only those familiar with his ceaseless thirst for change could have predicted the suddenness with which he ditched the last remnants of Ziggy and ushered in a new era characterised by sharp suits, a conventional haircut and sensible shoes. It was a radical transformation, and one that finally enabled him to crack America. Sizeable pockets of Bowie Boys kept the faith in Britain, fans whose influence would rebound several years later with the New Romantic movement.

Bowie plays Ziggy just one more time. Performing 'Dodo' on NBC's *Midnight Special* TV show, October 1973.

But first there was some unfinished Ziggy business. A lapse in inspiration, coupled with legal wrangles over a song publishing contract with Chrysalis Music, resulted in Bowie's nostalgic trip back to Swinging London for *Pin Ups*, an affectionate if unsatisfying collection of cover versions. The move certainly took the heat out of Bowiemania, and with the news that Mick Ronson had left at the end of the sessions, Bowie's rock'n'roll suicide seemed to be unfolding nicely.

Only now, it wasn't rock'n'roll; it was, shrieked Bowie, "Genocide!". Having squashed his Spiders, Bowie slid further into his own dark fantasies. He attempted to buy the rights to George Orwell's *1984*, a nightmarish portrait of totalitarianism, for a stage musical, but the author's widow blocked the move. He struck up a friendship with Beat novelist and gun-toting misanthrope William Burroughs. And he was enjoying the dubious benefits of cocaine. Bowie was indeed floating in a most peculiar way, and the changes were now coming faster than ever.

Pin Ups in Paris, July 1973. *Vogue* magazine commissioned a shot of Twiggy and Ziggy, by fashion snapper Justin de Villeneuve, who recalls: "Bowie would have been the first man ever on the cover. He loved the idea. When Bowie saw the finished picture he asked if he could use it for his album. I owned the picture, so I decided to let him have it. *Vogue* didn't talk to me for years after, they were very angry."

With *Diamond Dogs*, his "glam apocalypse" album released in 1974, Ziggy (at least what looked like a beastified version of him on the cover) was rescued from mid-Sixties London and dumped in the vaguely futuristic Hunger City, a bleak urban landscape overrun by sinister urchins and lethal canines. As the record unfolded, the scenario transformed into one of post-apocalyptic desolation. Bowie allowed his dystopian dreams to run wild, a manifestation of a lifelong fascination with power and death. "This album is more me than anything I've done previously," Bowie insisted. He wasn't joking.

The accompanying *Diamond Dogs* show was taken to America, land of love and hate, and the main inspiration for Bowie's panoramic visions of social breakdown. Any question that Ziggy came too was soon banished by the sight of Bowie in a neatly-pressed Yves St Laurent suit and smart, layered hair with a hitherto unfashionable side-parting. The sight of this latter-day crooner (Lester Bangs described him as "Johnny Ray on cocaine singing about 1984") performing what was virtually a one-man show to stardust-encrusted audiences chanting "We want Ziggy!" was awesome enough, but even that was outflanked by what was regarded at the time as the most spectacular rock show ever staged – though not everyone agreed that it had much to do with rock.

Mad Dogs And Englishmen. In this breathtaking photograph by Terry O' Neill, Bowie dons a Spanish hat.

Dog Man Star

Facing page: "To this day he was the most extreme. Bowie got away with wearing things that looked stupid on others. In this period he really did look like an alien, like no one else."
- Adam Ant.

Tony Visconti remembers: "I was there the night when the cherry-picker got stuck during 'Space Oddity', and David had to crawl back down the pole. The fans were trying to grab his bottom and his clothes, and he made it look like it was part of the act!"

With a choreographer, Toni Basil, and a classically trained Musical Director, Michael Kamen, it was as if Broadway had sneaked up on rock'n'roll and stole its heart. It was a slick and genuinely awe-inspiring spectacle, though the night when the hydraulic arm played up, leaving Bowie suspended in mid-air for half-a-dozen songs, provided amusing relief for the increasingly embittered session men forced to perform in the shadows for minimal wages.

The black music influence that had been detectable on parts of *Diamond Dogs*, most notably on the superfunk-charged '1984' and the soul ballad, 'Rock'n'Roll With Me', intoxicated Bowie during his latest American visit. With Ava Cherry his regular companion, he saw James Brown at the Apollo, The Jackson 5 at Madison Square Garden and began to frequent the new disco clubs. When, during a break in the tour, Bowie wanted to record again, Ava came up with the Sigma Sound Studios in Philadelphia. This was the home of the Philly Sound, created by Kenny Gamble and Leon Huff, whose artists included the O Jays, Billy Paul, Harold Melvin and The Bluenotes and The Three Degrees.

Bowie had tried grand-scale rock theatre at the Rainbow shows in August 1972, but usually the theatricality of his shows relied on his costume changes. The Diamond Dogs tour was different. With little expense spared, Bowie employed Broadway lighting man Jules Fisher and designer Mark Ravitz to transform the stage into Hunger City, with instructions that it should draw on expressionist films like *Metropolis* and *The Cabinet Of Dr Caligari*, with a bit of Albert Speer (the architect of the Third Reich) thrown in. Watchtowers, alleys, bridges, beams, a boxing-ring, a giant hand, even a 70-foot hydraulic arm which raised Bowie high above the audience, were cradled by two giant skyscrapers on either side of the stage. Three trucks were required to transport the set around the country.

"Ever since I started working with Carlos Alomar in 1974, I've found writing within the context of American soul and R&B the most exciting way of writing for me." Rhythm maestro Alomar went on to be Musical Director for a further four Bowie tours, and the pair were reunited in 1995 on the Outside tour (*above*) on which Bowie wears a Todd Oldham shirt.

"Tony Basil taught him things like 'Don't ever waste a movement. If you have to put your microphone down, do it with a flourish. If you have to walk from one side of the stage to the other, do it with great dramatic gestures. Throw your head back before you put your first step out'." - Tony Visconti.

The skeletal *Live*
cover: David Bowie Is
Alive And Well And
Living Only In Theory

Never mind the quality, feel
the width. In almost any
situation, Bowie has always
been able to hold his own.

Slinky Vagabond. For his new
'soul tour' in late 1974,
Bowie went Puerto Rican-
style, with box jackets,
pegged trousers and a thigh
chain the order of the day.

The Mask. Performing
'Aladdin Sane' in West
Virginia, June 1974.

With the producers' MFSB house band on another engagement, Bowie hired some of the best black session players around and began to lay the basis of his most radical musical transformation yet. The resulting *Young Americans* album was, he said, his "Plastic soul" take on the sounds of young black America.

The strangest man in rock'n'roll had, by a mixture of design and good fortune, sanitised the sound of its black cities for a white-bread audience. It was shamelessly opportunist and pleasantly perverse, a genuine gamble presented as a fait accompli. Bowie even started selling records in the States, and in spring 1975, 'Fame' (which at least was thematically consistent if nothing else) gave him his first No. 1 single.

This quickfire style makeover also affected the tour. The set that had dominated the early dates was abandoned. The band was reshuffled with guitarist Carlos Alomar, drummer Dennis Davis and backing singer Luther Vandross drafted in to reflect the new direction. Now, Bowie and his band performed on a bare stage against a simple white backdrop. Back home, the reaction was muted, though Bowie's foppish new 'wedge' haircut with orange tint and blond streaks, helped inspire the new Soul Boy culture. Not all these enthusiasts followed his next move, but they provided a vital link between the Northern Soul scene and the emerging disco culture. And the man in the outsized zoot suit? "Alive and well and living in theory," he reckoned with the benefit of hindsight.

With John & Yoko, and
some not so young
Americans (Simon and
Garfunkel, Roberta Flack)
at the Grammy Awards,
New York, March 1975.

Facing page: The wedge cut -
Phil Oakey was intrigued.

LIKE A ROLLING CLONE

Bowie's success, and his enduring appeal, has been an inspiration to many artists in search of an old idea. Some of these Bowie clones were well-intentioned, many plain daft, but they tend to disprove the theory that all blokes look wonderful in make-up.

"In my early stuff I made it through on sheer pretension. I consider myself responsible for a whole new school of pretensions."

Bauhaus
Oh dear. Punk met Glam and spawned a Goth monster, and they rarely came more hackneyed than Bauhaus, fronted by pouting Pete Murphy. Still, the band achieved something Bowie's not done – taken 'Ziggy Stardust' into the UK singles chart. Well, it was 1982.

Jobriath
"I can do better than that!" Record company mogul David Geffen threw half a million quid at *Hair* star Bruce Campbell (*above*), changed his name to the spookily alien Jobriath, spent another million hyping the 'American Bowie' with a spectacular campaign (no interviews, no decent songs), then watched helplessly as the rise and fall of Jobriath stalled at the bargain-bin.

Bob Dylan
Judas! Even Bob Dylan, that sacred cow of pre-Glam authenticity, slapped on the pancake and began referring to himself as "Jokerman".

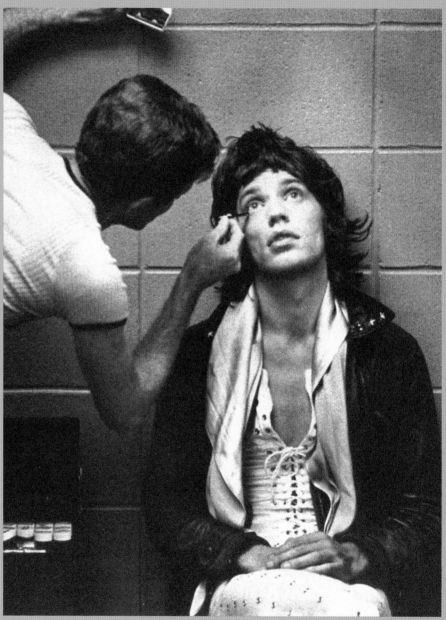

Mick Jagger
The head Stone was paranoid that his new Chelsea neighbour might pinch some of his ideas. Of course, this rhinestone jumpsuit and eyeliner look, worn during the Stones' 1973 tour, owed nothing to Bowie at all.

Japan
David Batt enjoyed the "crashing out with Sylvian" line in 'Drive-In Saturday' so much that he nabbed a new surname from it. David Sylvian then formed Japan just so people might refer to him as "some cat from Japan" (from 'Ziggy Stardust'). Japan generally steered clear of Bowie's music thereafter, but if the look was *Young Americans*, the attitude was pure *The Man Who Fell To Earth*.

Gary Numan
A hero, just for one day.

Sweet
These brickies-in-satin outdid the Artful One just once, when 'Blockbuster', a spoiler that used the same riff as 'The Jean Genie', went one better than Bowie's hit reaching No.1 early in 1973.

Babylon Zoo
Like Bowie's first hit, the Bab Zoo's 1996 single 'Spaceman' was a 'once heard, never forgotten' record. Unlike Bowie, they've yet to experience a rebirth.

Leo Sayer
Before tosh like 'When I Need You', Leo Sayer was a warm-up act for Roxy Music who dressed in a Pierrot costume, waved his hands in a manner that suggested his straitjacket was undone, and told interviewers that the true meaning of a clown was "the sadness behind". He soon left the clown costume behind, but unfortunately the sadness remained.

Sigue Sigue Sputnik
The Sputniks had a winning formula. The image was circa '73 Bowie mangled through punk and cyber-movies. The scam, screw EMI for loadsa-money, was The Sex Pistols all over again. And the outcome? A genuine case of from ashes to ashes.

Psychedelic Furs
Richard Butler thought he was the real Eighties David Bowie. But nobody else did (though Bowie was apparently impressed).

Stardust
This golden turkey, which went into production shortly after Ziggy's retirement in 1973, chronicled the rise and fall of a pop star. Its star has risen considerably since the release of Todd Haynes' revisionist Glam movie, *Velvet Goldmine*.

They'll never clone ya! "I find it ironic when I look at a band like Sigue Sigue Sputnik (*above*), where it's so outré, so absolutely in the Ziggy court. All this time later, it still raises its brightly coloured head."

Not many people needed Leo Sayer (*above*). Bowie: "We were very miffed that people who had obviously never seen *Metropolis* and had never heard of Christopher Isherwood were actually becoming glam rockers."

"I was in no state to be responsible. I was the least responsible person that I can imagine at that time."

2.4

Thin White Duke

Bowie's costumes may have become more sober as the decade progressed, but controversy was rarely far away. On May 2, 1976, he returned home for the first time in nearly two years, arriving at London's Victoria Station in a specially chartered train from Dover. It was a stage-managed, meet-the-fans kind of occasion, designed to publicise his forthcoming six-night stint at London's Empire Pool. Alighting the train, David stepped into an open-top Mercedes and remained upright while technicians fiddled with a faulty PA system.

Bowie gets ready to 'wave' to the faithful. Gary Numan was there: "I didn't see anyone walking around saying, 'What a wanker, he did a Nazi salute'. No one. People just thought he was waving at them, and I'm sure he was."

Gone was the baggy, American-style formalwear favoured by New York clubgoers and provincial Soul Boys. Instead, as he'd declared at the start of his latest album, *Station To Station*, he'd returned as the Thin White Duke – a faintly archaic, austere and avowedly European character dressed in a black shirt and tight, functional jeans. His slicked-back hair, streaked with blond, appeared to have prematurely aged him. He then 'waved' to his fans. Thirty years earlier, the gesture, which would almost certainly have been described as a Nazi salute. Was pop's master of propaganda now overstepping the mark in allowing his private obsessions to become a public nuisance?

Facing page: Fashion! Turn to the right. Bowie: "The right wing politics thing was just bullshit, something I said off the cuff."

('Word On A Wing'). And the Thin White Duke was "throwing darts in lovers' eyes". Poisonous ones. Bowie wasn't a fascist or a racist. He was a cultural pessimist with a wicked streak of misanthropy that, if anything, had been reinforced by his rock star experiences. Elitism was built into the star/fan equation; audiences could be manipulated with consummate ease. But neither stars, nor the media that provides the link between them and their audiences, could ever admit as much. And, besides, Bowie was feeling bored and truculent. "The rock business has become so established, and so much like a society, that I have revolted against it. That's what wasn't liked – that I won't take it seriously, and I'll break its rules, and I won't listen to it, and I won't take much notice of it. It doesn't worry me." He returned to his Nietzsche and Crowley texts, built up a tidy library on all aspects of the Third Reich... and began to talk.

The 1976 shows were stark and Expressionistic; beams of white light cast dark shadows and created an air of malevolence. Bowie's usual stage-wear – crisp white shirt, black waistcoat and tapered trousers – was his most functional yet but disarmingly effective, though his detached star persona seemed more pronounced than ever. The props had gone, but Bowie now insisted that less is more. "It's more theatrical than *Diamond Dogs* ever was," he said. "(But) it's by suggestion rather than over-propping. It relies on modern, 20th century concepts of lighting and I think it comes over as very theatrical... It doesn't look like a theatrical presentation, but it certainly is."

Even his music had cooled. On *Station To Station*, Bowie had ditched the slick Stateside sounds of *Young Americans* for a more sober, continental style inspired by electric Krautrock rhythms ('TVC15') and the Euro-ballad tradition

BOWIEPHILES

Cameras In Brooklyn.

How Lucky You Are. Fans who 'asked for an autograph' are rewarded for their perseverence.

Decked out like a Christmas tree.

Audiences who dressed like their idols were a rare breed before Ziggy Stardust. The odd Elvis or Jagger lookalike might have lurked in the shadows, but fans usually showed their appreciation in the time-honoured fashion of pinning posters on bedroom walls or waving hastily-scrawled placards. Bowie, via Ziggy's comic-book look, inspired a rash of lookalikes, many of whom (the 'Bowie Boys') mimicked his each and every stylistic change throughout the Seventies. It's worth noting that enthusiasm for Glass Spider suits or Black Tie White Noise chic during the past two decades has been muted.

The Bowie cult was remarkable in that it constituted an entire subculture centred on a single personality. When *Cracked Actor* director Alan Yentob asked a fan if he was "into the Bowie universe", the response ("He's the centre: I was drawn to it") was uttered in the manner of a religious doctrine. There was a mild moral panic when, in 1973, the more daring Bowie Boys (and Girls) began turning up at school sporting Ziggy-styled mullets. Like smoking, long hair and pen-knives, David Bowie had become every head teacher's nightmare.

"I've never seen such a strange gathering of people," wrote one *Melody Maker* reporter of a Ziggy-era Bowie crowd. "For a start there were many people who resembled Christmas trees on legs. There was much glitter, and several men dressed as ladies." Following Bowie fashions was never quite as troublesome again, although his audiences still seem to make a bit of an effort when he comes to town.

Bowie didn't merely inspire copycats. The young Billy Idol was one of the Bromley Contingent, a group of early punk enthusiasts who saw no contradiction in watching The Sex Pistols one night, and Bowie doing his Thin White Duke routine the next. "We liked to be noticed," he told *England's Dreaming* author Jon Savage. "We were influenced by Bowie, Roxy and *Clockwork Orange* but we were doing it in our own way. Bowie had dyed his hair red, but we went into a hairdressers and saw all these tubes of crazy colour and went mad."

Facing page: "The audiences are always about one tour behind me, but then they always were. I'd get worried if they turned up in outfits that I'd never seen before. I'd think I was a tour behind."

"For about a year I tried to look like Bowie, but it never happened for me, unfortunately. For a very short period I had the Thin White Duke look. I used to wear the waistcoat and I had the blond bit at the front of my hair."
- Gary Numan.

Duke Of Earl. Bowie had recorded a version of the Gene Chandler classic with The Mannish Boys more than 20 years before this photo was taken.

The headlines soon began to pile up. "The best thing to happen is for an extreme right government to come." "I'd adore to be Prime Minister. And, yes, I believe very strongly in fascism... People have always responded with greater efficiency under a regimental leadership." "Rock stars are fascists too. Adolf Hitler was one of the first rock stars. I think he was quite as good as Jagger. And, boy, when he hit that stage, he worked an audience." "(Ziggy) could have been Hitler in England... I think I might have been a bloody good Hitler. I'd be an excellent dictator. Very eccentric and quite mad."

Later that summer, Eric Clapton interrupted a concert in Birmingham to advocate the repatriation policies of the Ulster Unionist MP Enoch Powell. It proved the last straw for a handful of activists who, after a vigorous letter-writing campaign in the music press, founded Rock Against Racism (RAR) to stem pop's swing to the far right. One of their pamphlets pictured Bowie's face alongside Powell's.

The politics of fear fed off the sense of imminent crisis that gripped mid-Seventies Britain. The economy was in a mess, the workers were getting restless and social disorder didn't seem very far off. The chattering classes could find no easy solution, but they certainly didn't welcome glib and inflammatory statements from rock stars. Ultimately, though, it wasn't really Bowie they feared but the people out in the blue-collar heartlands, the ones who were starting to vote National Front in bi-elections, who tended to seek their scapegoats first and ask questions later.

Bowie, too, was motivated by fear of the masses more than any love for the ideology of fascism: "People aren't very bright, you know. They say they want freedom, but when they get the chance, they pass up Nietzsche and choose Hitler, because he would march into a room to speak and music and lights would come on at strategic moments." His elitism was shameless, but the real tragedy was that the thrust of his argument wasn't necessarily untrue.

"I thought he looked coolest around *Station To Station*, but it wasn't so much the clothes - it was his hair, his face, just the elegance of it." - Iggy Pop.

"I'd got this thing in my mind that I was through with theatrical clothes and I would only wear Sears & Roebuck. Which on me looked more outlandish than anything I had made by Japanese designers."

Facing page: "I hadn't liked the non-eyebrow period, which basically went from *Aladdin Sane* to *Young Americans*. Then he got the eyebrows back, and his hair was fantastic in *The Man Who Fell To Earth* and thus rekindled my wanting to be David Bowie again."
- Ian McCulloch.

At a VIP gala premiere of *The Man Who Fell To Earth* with Sydne Rome at the Gaumont Elysees Theatre, Paris, June 1977.

2.5

Punk Pierrot

Punk was Bowie's Shock Rock writ large. Not since the *Ziggy Stardust / Aladdin Sane* era had rock experienced such an outbreak of extravagant fashions and exaggerated personalities. It was as if the next generation had digested Bowie's pet obsessions – identity, gender confusion, morbid curiosity – and spewed them out again in even greater displays of flamboyance and outrage.

She Shook Me Cold. "He had a big influence on that old boot Siouxsie. She was just a Bowie fan, she was never into the punk side of things." - Captain Sensible of The Damned.

If his Thin White Duke routine had cast David Bowie further adrift from the rock mainstream, it soon began to work in his favour. Technically, Bowie, who'd turned 30 in January 1977, was a fully paid-up 'Old Fart', but his eternal outcast status demanded that he not be put out to pasture just yet. After all, many of the new, so-called Blank Generation (shades of Warhol there) had been reared on a Bowie-sanctioned diet of Velvet Underground, Iggy Pop and the death-wish star supremo, Ziggy Stardust. One of the new acts, Siouxsie and The Banshees, had virtually come into being at one of Bowie's Station to Station Wembley shows.

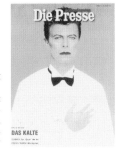

Cabaret, 1991: "This was based on a businessman I saw walking to work one morning in Berlin. He had his briefcase, and a suit and tie on - not a dickie bow - very traditional, apart from this bright red lipstick. I stored the image in my head for years!"

BOWIE STYLE

This Ziggy-era reissue of Bowie's 1969 LP pre-dated Lydon's late Seventies look by five years. David: "Oh, if Ziggy Stardust had had a son. When Ziggy fell from favour and lost all his money, he had a son before he died… Johnny Rotten!"

Punk's rude interruption carried distinct echoes of Bowie's arrival in 1972. The Swindle, Malcolm McLaren's 10-point dissection of The Sex Pistols' mission to destroy the record industry, was a naughtier version of MainMan's scams couched in manifesto form. (The first lesson was "How To Manufacture Your Group.") The Spiders weren't exactly one-chord wonders, but like punk, they offended trad rock sensibilities with vibrant, cutting-edge chords and unfussy rhythms. More important still, punk's revived sense of carnival – with obvious sexual and anti-social overtones – owed much to Ziggy's dashing cocktail of *A Clockwork Orange* and Warhol's Factory Superstars. With hundreds of aliases – Johnny Rotten, Polly Styrene, Rat Scabies et al – on the loose, it was as if Glam Rock had returned having made a pact with the devil.

Bowie wisely maintained a low profile during the early months of punk. He spent much of his time in Berlin, the ideal haunt for resuming a life of artful debauchery with his constant companion and similarly acclaimed Godfather Of Punk, Iggy Pop.

Bowie's punk-era albums *Low* and *"Heroes"* (both 1977) forged new ground, although not all of his old admirers welcomed his experimentally inclined robotic cabaret routine: "(*Low*) stinks of artfully counterfeited spiritual descent and emptiness," was Charles Shaar Murray's verdict. Nevertheless, they won him a new, left-field audience (encouraged by the involvement of Eno and Robert Fripp), and compared favourably with, say, Bryan Ferry's Casanova conceits. One ad published around the time of *Heroes* cleverly sought to remove Bowie from the style wars: "There's Old Wave, There's New Wave. And then there's David Bowie".

The Henna-haired little wonder: Bowie returned to punky orange spikes in 1997.

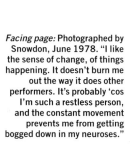

Facing page: Photographed by Snowdon, June 1978. "I like the sense of change, of things happening. It doesn't burn me out the way it does other performers. It's probably 'cos I'm such a restless person, and the constant movement prevents me from getting bogged down in my neuroses."

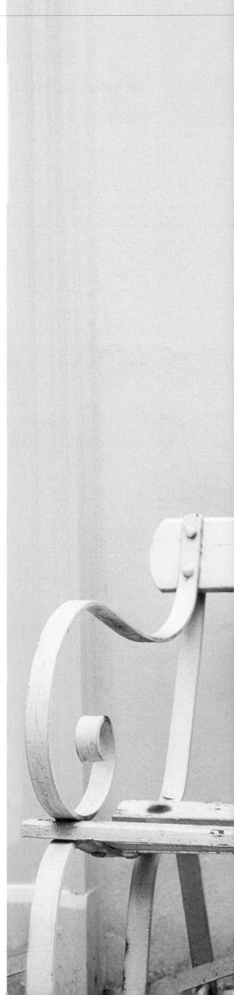

In March 1978, Bowie made his move. He gambled on a huge world tour, and had the good sense to restore a good percentage of Ziggy Stardust material into his set. (A 'Ziggy Lives' banner was draped over a balcony at Earl's Court in appreciation.) His usual costumes were pitched at two dominant subcultures: a squeaky clean white outfit, gaily set off with a sailor's cap, favoured by disco audiences; and the tight-fitting tops and punkish trousers of the new wave. The shows were cautionary, cabaret-like affairs intended to please the diehards and placate the cynics. With Bowie enviably preserved, and performing against a seedy neon backdrop, it just about worked.

The late Seventies were incredibly kind to David Bowie. Punk opened many doors, including one for a bunch of synthesizer-brandishing amateurs with steely gazes and lop-sided haircuts. Dubbed the Cold Wave, these artful experimentalists often appeared caught between Bowie's shocking presentation of old (the Human League's Phil Oakey sported two hairstyles on one head) and the eerie electronic mood-pieces of his recent work.

Two further albums, *Lodger* (1979) and *Scary Monsters (And Super Creeps)* (1980) kept him at the outer limits of the mainstream, but it was one of those visual masterstrokes that nursed him back to full critical and commercial health.

The tour's mixed reception had concerned Bowie. A video for a 1979 single, 'Boys Keep Swinging', put him back in women's clothes – and on screen – again. Musically, he was fresh, too: both 'Boys' and 'Look Back In Anger', sounded as contemporary as anything else that year. A version

of Brecht/Weill's 'Alabama Song' released in 1980 beat the new iconoclasts at their own game – it was the musical equivalent of a drunken brawl. But it was the follow-up, 'Ashes To Ashes', that really caught the public's imagination. Magnificently self-referential, infused with melancholy, stunningly arranged and with an irresistibly understated hook, it was 'Space Oddity' all grown up. It dominated the entire summer.

In the accompanying video, Bowie returned to some core themes – alien landscapes, madness and gender confusion – with costumes to suit. But it was his updated Pierrot outfit, designed by Natasha Kornilof, that eclipsed everything else. Bang on cue, Bowie had tapped into a flamboyant new scene centred on the Blitz club in Holborn, London, co-opting a handful of its leading faces, including the club's co-owner Steve Strange, for the video.

Swing your pants.

In kimono with actor Peter Straker, at the London premiere party for *Just A Gigolo*, Valentine's Day 1979.

Facing page: "The point is to grow into the person you grow into. I haven't a clue where I'm gonna be in a year. A raving nut, a flower child or a dictator, some kind of reverend. I don't know. That's what keeps me from getting bored."

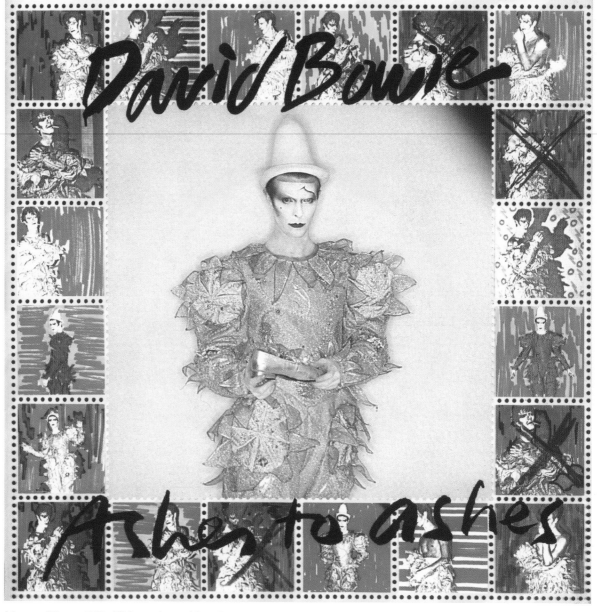

David Bowie
Ashes to ashes

Below: I was stone and he was wax. "I've still got that mannequin at home, you know."

Many of these Blitz Kids, or later, New Romantics, had been aspiring wedge-headed Soul Boys during the mid-Seventies. Now, having come of age, they were dedicated to a way of life that revolved around gender-bending and club culture hedonism. Punk had pogoed itself to death; the independent scene had come over all earnest. The Blitz crowd – with transvestite Marilyn on the door, Boy George swanning around the crowd and Spandau Ballet on stage – wanted only fun and the freedom to create jaw-dropping new guises for themselves on a nightly basis.

By the end of 1980, Bowie had made it onto the cover of the new style bible, *The Face*. His confidence had been restored to such an extent that he could even afford a gentle dig at all his young pretenders: "One of the new wave boys… same old thing in brand new drag" ('Teenage Wildlife'). He could also add a new entry to his extensive list of credits: survivor.

Following pages: Costumes and comments by Natasha Kornilof: "The clown was based on a Jacobean costume with big padded trousers and sleeves. It was layer-upon-layer of blue shiny fabric with silk organza and braid over that. And silver net over blue lurex."

"I was amazingly gratified with the white trousers, which were cut like Jacobean trousers. I couldn't believe I'd just changed the shape of what everyone was wearing. All the Futurists and New Romantics came from that." And MC Hammer.

"I think (music) should be tarted up, made into a prostitute, a parody of itself. It should be the clown, the Pierrot medium."

Facing page: 'TVC 15'. In pencil skirt uniform for *Saturday Night Live*, New York, December 1979, Bowie's "Communist Chinese air-hostess look", designed by Natasha Kornilof.

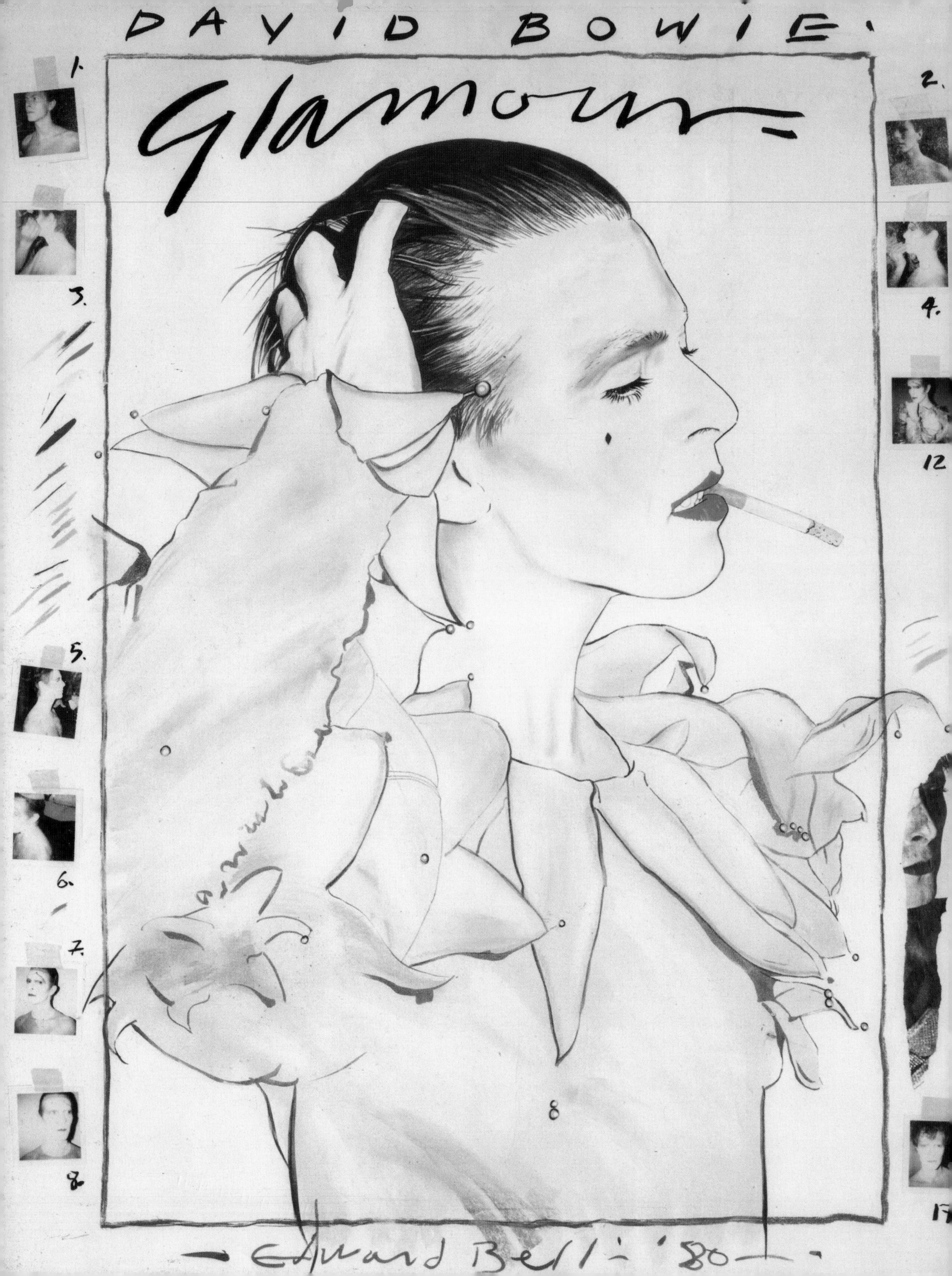
DAVID BOWIE
Glamour
Edward Bell '80

Come Fly With Me. On stage
during a Serious Moonlight
show at the 60,000 capacity
Milton Keynes Bowl,
England, July 2, 1983.

3.1

I'm Only Dancing

*For two decades, Bowie had stayed ahead of –
or at least abreast with – the pack thanks to his
uncanny ability to sniff out emerging trends and
give them his own spin. During the Eighties and
Nineties, his instincts proved as sharp as ever.
He played huge stadium extravaganzas when
everyone temporarily forgot they were naff,
and hung out in tiny drum & bass clubs when
he wanted to remind audiences of his cultish
disposition. The vision and sounds kept moving
on, but something fundamental had changed:
it's as if the David Bowie that re-emerged in 1983
had erased huge chunks of his past. It's only in
recent years that he's been able to 'rewind' again,
evidence that, beneath the masks and the guises,
David Bowie has finally achieved his ultimate
creation – that of a well-rounded, multi-faceted
and essentially contented character.*

As the new decade began, Bowie's record sales
were higher than ever and his critical reputation
in rude health. Punk's defiantly 'anti' stance was
looking tired in the face of the New Romantics,
and the aggressively upbeat "Go For It!" culture
that was being nurtured by the Thatcher admin-
istration. Where punk had once threatened the
very fabric of popular music, its woeful lack of
staying power and quickly compromised ideals
provoked a reaction that amounted to a virtual
amnesty for the old guard. David Bowie was voted
Best Male Singer by *NME* readers at the start of
1982 despite having done virtually nothing the
previous year. Phil Collins started 'shifting units' in
vast quantities. It was, as all the cynics agreed,
"Like Punk Never Happened".

Facing page: Come Blow
Your Horn. On stage
during a special fan club
gig at the 600-capacity
Hanover Grand, London,
June 2, 1997.

PROTÉGÉS

Iggy Pop remembers his *Raw Power*: "I think the little touches Bowie put on the mix helped, and I think some of the things MainMan did helped, and more than anything else, what the whole experience did was to get me out of Detroit and onto a world stage."

Proof that the deification of David Bowie in 1972-73 was not necessarily misplaced came when nearly every struggling artist that brushed past him in a studio suddenly enjoyed a revival of fortunes.

Arnold Corns
Bowie's Fairy Godmother touch took time to nurture. His first stab at building a family of like-minded talents around him stalled at the first hurdle when Arnold Corns, who he proclaimed would be bigger than The Rolling Stones, failed after one measly single. The band was basically a dry run for the Spiders, with Bowie's dress designer Freddi Burretti sharing the vocals.

With Freddi Burretti, 1971. Bowie: "Freddi was a very straight sort of queen. He took one look and screamed, 'I can't wear that!'. It took me all day to get him into that dress."

Iggy Pop
Iggy Pop had thrown up on stage one too many times for Elektra Records executives. His band The Stooges were dropped in summer 1971 and the music biz shed few tears. Bowie admired Iggy's destructive persona and unrelenting Detroit rock; he instructed Tony DeFries to get The Stooges a new deal and bring them over to the UK where Bowie would advise them. The result was *Raw Power*, brilliant but half-smothered by Bowie's misguided attempt to get an authentic subterranean sound. It sold few copies, but Ig's legend was assured.

Mott The Hoople
Bowie's auteurist ambitions were advanced considerably when, in mid-1972, he dragged the hapless Mott The Hoople out of semi-retirement to record a song he'd just written, 'All The Young Dudes'. Within weeks, the band had a record deal and a Top 3 hit; and the *Clockwork Orange* generation had an anthem that underscored Bowie's Ziggy philosophy – with its coded references to drugs, cross-dressing and suicide. Bowie produced a tie-in album and the band's fortunes were transformed.

Mott mainman Ian Hunter insists: "I never saw anything sexual about 'Dudes' as a lyric. To me it was just a great song. After 'Dudes' we were considered instant fags. It was comical. I met some incredible folk."

Lou Reed
Reed was another underground legend with a bad attitude who owed his rehabilitation to Bowie. For a while, Reed was grateful, claiming that Bowie was "the only interesting person around. Everything has been tedious, rock'n'roll has been tedious, except for what David has been doing. There's a mutual empathy between us." After finishing work on the Mott album, Bowie and Ronson produced *Transformer* for Reed; one song, 'Walk On The Wild Side', gave the one-time Velvet Underground monotone man a British chart hit. Was there no limit to Bowie's sorcery?

Though *Transformer* is regarded by newer converts as the home of the original 'Perfect Day', for many the LP will be remembered as a classic glam experience. However, Lou Reed plays it way down: "A lot of it reminded me of when I was with Warhol. It was just that more people were doing it. Then it became stylised and commercialised. When that happened, it became nothing."

The Astronettes

During 1973, Bowie had been conducting an affair with his very own young American, Ava Cherry. Ava was one of a trio of Astronettes that occasionally danced and sang backing vocals at the more prestigious Bowie shows, and that summer, the singer decided she would be his next star. Unfortunately, the task proved to be more difficult than he'd imagined, not least because the Spiders were splitting and Bowie was suffering from burn-out. The project was still-born – though the unfinished tapes were released years later as *People From Bad Homes.*

Lulu

Bowie's success with women on an informal level was rarely matched in the studio, excepting a brief collaboration with Lulu. When they first met, in the mid-Sixties, she was hot property and he a virtual squatter outside the gates of pop's impenetrable fortress. By 1974, things had changed; Lulu was the outsider, a small screen celebrity who appeared to have squandered her vocal talents. Bowie offered her 'The Man Who Sold The World', produced the session and played sax on the record. Despite a hilarious dance routine, Lulu enjoyed the heady heights of Top Three success once again, but her revival in fortunes was brief.

Dana Gillespie

Bowie was involved in two songs on Dana Gillespie's *Weren't Born A Man* LP, released in 1974, but neither that, nor Dana's obvious sexual charms, played to the hilt in the publicity campaign, could save the record. Thoughts of making Amanda Lear or Wayne/Jayne County MainMan stars were quickly reconsidered.

Lulu performing 'The Man Who Sold The World' on German TV, 1974: "Lulu and I did a whole bunch of stuff that I thought had been lost. What we found recently was a really wonderful version of 'Can You Hear Me'. I would love to try and get this released, I think it would be quite beautiful."

'China Girl' video shoot in the Australian outback, (*right*) 1983.

Facing page: Announcing his plans for Eighties domination throughout the nation in a Georgian suite at London's Claridges hotel, March 1983: "I've learned to relax and be my present age and my present position. I feel comfortable in my mid-thirties. It doesn't seem such an alien place to be."

"My wife says that David wears clothes better than almost any man since Fred Astaire." - film director John Landis.

Bowie, who positioned the very idea of stardom at the centre of his art, had always felt under siege, despite the protective shells of Ziggy, the Thin White Duke, et al. The intense fan worship he'd inspired worldwide inevitably attracted its fair share of cranks, most of whom, if the Vermorels' *Starlust* book is anything to go by, indulged in harmless sexual fantasies. But since his teenage years, Bowie had often associated stardom with death, or at least decay, a suspicion that manifested itself publicly with Ziggy's 'Rock'n'Roll Suicide' and his shopping-list of phobias about flying and staying in tall hotels.

Bowie, had undergone a complete transformation during a two-year retreat between 1981 and 1983, and was perfectly poised to embrace the new pop-lite culture. His previous album, *Scary Monsters (And Super Creeps)*, had been the last under the terms of the old MainMan/RCA contract. That was incentive enough to crack a huge market with the next one. There was also the matter of John Lennon's death which, along with the Sharon Tate killing in 1969, had sent a grim reminder to celebrities that their status made them extremely vulnerable.

"If anything, maybe I've helped establish that rock 'n' roll is a pose."

With Keith Richards in New York.

Facing page: A conservative-looking Bowie with not so tasty 'scrambled egg' hair-do, 1983.

Showing off his star on the Hollywood Walk Of Fame, 1997. Many of Bowie's subsequent activities have been on the World Wide Web. BowieNet was launched in 1998, followed by BowieBanc.com, David's own online banking service, in 2000.

When Bowie re-emerged in 1983 for the *Let's Dance* album and world tour, he was a picture of health – bronzed, bleached, 'scrambled egg' hair, and with a permanent grin. On one level, it was simply the latest in a series of makeovers, one that picked up from his *Young Americans* look of 1975. Like punk never happened, indeed. At a deeper level, it marked a necessary retreat from the complex characters of the Seventies. Like the wider world at large, Bowie was playing safe, reducing the margin of error, in a quest for self-preservation that had been unfamiliar to him since the early Seventies. David Bowie was indeed alive and well and hoping to keep it that way. He even changed his brand of cigarettes.

This break with the past was largely prompted by the events of December 8, 1980, when John Lennon was shot dead by a fan who claimed that 'his' star had let him

down. For Bowie, who'd spent a large chunk of his career musing on the true meaning of stardom, often relating it to death, or at least personal collapse, the murder of a close friend who just happened to be one of the most famous men in the world hit him harder than he's ever let on. The effect was cataclysmic: it was as if the fatal shots had finally freed him from the self-destructive route his works had taken him. It was a filthy lesson, but an important spell had been broken.

Within hours of Lennon's death, Bowie had stepped up security at the Booth Theatre on Broadway in New York, where his portrayal of John Merrick, the so-called Elephant Man, had critics searching for new superlatives. Days later, he decided to end the run prematurely, spent Christmas with his mother for the first time in years, and then retreated to his Swiss residence. And, apart from venturing out for a

couple of acting roles, that's where he remained for the next year or so, until he was ready to face the most difficult role of his career – leaving all the disguises and neuroses behind and coming out as a rather less complicated David Bowie.

The final night of Bowie's extensive 1983 'comeback' tour closed in Hong Kong on the third anniversary of Lennon's death. It was a coincidence, but Bowie had been alerted to it a few days beforehand, and he came prepared. He told the audience that his last hours with the ex-Beatle were spent in Hong Kong. "I saw a Beatle jacket on a stall and asked him to put it on so that I could take a photograph," he said. Holding back the tears, in a rare public display of emotion, Bowie then launched into a version of Lennon's 'Imagine'.

On the run from the style police: 'I'm Afraid Of Americans' in New York, 1997.

Distraught Beatles fans gather outside the Dakota Building in New York, 1980.

In his dual 'Blue Jean' role as the nerdish Vic, Bowie tried to tempt fellow style merchant and Seventies rival, Bryan Ferry, into the role of his well-dressed flatmate.

Perfoming 'Golden Years' in 1983: "That's one of my favourite songs of his. It's a direct descendent of 'Happy Years', a Fifties single by The Diamonds." - Mannish Boy, Bob Solly.

This clean slate was reflected in his Bowie's music and stage presentation. *Let's Dance* was slick and upbeat, bearing all the sophisticated dancefloor trademarks of Chic's producer Nile Rodgers. The tie-in Serious Moonlight tour, which lasted seven months, was conducted on a grand scale, with Mark Ravitz, a veteran from the *Diamond Dogs* shows, returning to supervise the sets. The musicians were casually dressed in the manner of a Fifties Hong Kong bar band; Bowie in his pastel-coloured suits, shirt, tie and braces, looked more like a hip Wall Street businessman than the "magnificent outrage" of yore. He was pushing 40, still undeniably pretty and eager to show that he had the enthusiasm and bushy-tailed outlook of a spoilt teenager.

Rock in the mid-Eighties became sophisticated, ironic and fiercely individual. No one believed in purity anymore. The get-rich-quick philosophy was mirrored by a fame-at-any-price fix. The bastard offspring of David Bowie were everywhere, from Eurythmics and Scritti Politti in Britain, U2 in Ireland and Madonna and Talking Heads in America, though some were more clever than others. Certainly most were more financially astute than Bowie had once been. Unfortunately, not many of them were capable of making decent records because everyone was so overawed by technology and desperate not to appear behind the times that they handed over their music to the technobores who sat behind the mixing-desks. Unfortunately, there wasn't a Brian Eno amongst them.

"David Bowie really played with ideas, and iconography and imagery. He's a brilliant man. And a gentleman too." - Madonna.

Facing page:
Tonight (1984): Bowie portrays Screamin' Lord Byron in the video for the album's lead single, 'Blue Jean'.

'Under Pressure' with Annie Lennox, 1992. Eurythmics have covers of Bowie's 'Sound & Vision' and 'Fame' in their vaults. More recently, they closed their Millennium Concert with 'Life On Mars?'.

STAGECRAFT

Bowie revived 1974's memorable 'Cracked Actor' skullduggery with even greater success on the Serious Moonlight tour nine years later.

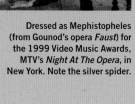

"I was trying to redefine my version of rock - personally, in the way that I felt it, as a more stage-oriented, theatrical kind of artist."

Bowie's achievement was to expose the fiction of that transparency, and to elevate rock theatre into an integral part of the experience.

Alice Cooper, persona non grata in the Bowie camp during the early Seventies, had set the ball rolling with his *Love It To Death* stage show that utilised weapons, a boa constrictor and a staged execution.

It was compelling rock theatre but, Bowie insisted, it had little to do with art.

Brian Eno is in no doubt where Bowie's true creative value lies: "He's one of the most important European musicians of the whole rock era. I think he introduced something that was always there, but was unstated and very unclearly articulated, which was this notion of theatricality – this idea of, 'Look, what we're doing is about theatre, it's not just about music.' Nobody had done it quite as artistically."

Bowie's sense of drama was not always so well defined. In the late Sixties, he wrote a television play, *The Champion Flower Grower*, and submitted it to the BBC. The response didn't make comfortable reading: "Mr. Bowie has really not yet begun to consider what a play is and this total lack of dramatic development just rules the script out." Wisely, he stuck to the occasional

walk-on part while he waited for the real plum role to arrive – playing David Bowie on the greatest stage of all.

Even without an avowed guise, Bowie has always "felt like an actor". That's how he credited himself on the *Hunky Dory* album in 1971; it's why his skull-wielding skit on Shakespeare's *Hamlet* on the Diamond Dogs tour was so memorable; and why he admired the camp, exaggerated personalities of Andy Warhol's court crazies. He was virtually required to play himself playing Aladdin Sane for *The Man Who Fell To Earth* in 1975, which was bags more fun than the majority of his subsequent 'proper' acting roles. But Bowie's theatricality was not about traditional acting roles but playing out something far more dramatic on the rock stage – where many felt it didn't belong.

Rock and theatre became irrevocably entwined the day Elvis Presley first shook his hips for American television. The cameraman was told to shoot from the waist up, and the persuasiveness of rock'n'roll's visual power was assured. Early British acts, such as Screaming Lord Sutch, with his long coloured hair, loin-cloth, monster feet and coffin, owed more to the vaudevillian tradition-ghoulish gimmicks performed for a giggle. Even the hippies demanded showbiz theatrics: that's why Jimi Hendrix had to set fire to his guitar, why no Hawkwind concert was complete without dancer Stacia parading her ample bosom (*below*).

Mostly, rock theatre was either transparent, like Mick Jagger's increasingly butch androgyny, or else played for laughs, like the Bonzo Dog Doo-Dah Band.

For Cooper, the role-playing ended as soon as the curtain went down.

Throughout 1971, Bowie had been telling interviewers that he was going to become "much more theatrical, more outrageous"; his shows would be "quite different to anything anyone else has tried to do before". "Entertainment (is) what's missing in pop music now," he maintained. "There's only me and Marc Bolan." By 1973, Ziggy and Aladdin had blurred the boundaries between rock and theatre, between play and role-play. The spectacle briefly took over during 1974, but for most of his career, Bowie has always applied a panoramic perspective to his live performances that drew not only from the European (and, later, Japanese) stage but to art cinema and the digital medium.

Dressed as Mephistopheles (from Gounod's opera *Faust*) for the 1999 Video Music Awards, MTV's *Night At The Opera*, in New York. Note the silver spider.

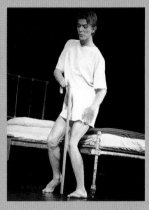

With Lindsay Kemp, 1973. "He introduced me to a lot of extraordinary things - Artaud, Theatre Of The Absurd, all that kind of thing. A lot of my attitude toward the stage, and staging, really came from Linsday. He was my mentor."

On Broadway: "The trouble is I always look for parts with an emotional or physical limp, and I always seem to get them."

Late in 1973, at a function to celebrate the work of Lindsay Kemp (*above*), Bowie said: "There's been a lot of talk over the past couple of years about rock theatre. Well, here's the man who started it all, with whom I spent two fantastic years learning and working."

Bowie later revived his Kemp-procured mime skills for the stage adaptation of *The Elephant Man* (*far right*) on Broadway to great critical acclaim.

For all his Pop Art iconoclasm, Bowie never lost his respect for the traditional theatrical arts.

After seeing the stage version of *Cabaret*, starring Judi Dench, which later became the inspiration for his 1976 shows, he said: "The stage lighting was phenomenal... What I didn't know is that it was Brechtian lighting. It was just stark white light, and I'd never seen that before in my life, and that became a central image for me, of what stage lighting should look like. I mean, I'd never seen it on a rock'n'roll stage."

Ultimately, Bowie believes that the power of theatre eclipses that of sound. Promoting his *Black Tie White Noise* album in 1993, he said: "The eyes are a lot hungrier than the ears, and I think that when something is presented at a theatrical level, that's the foremost impression that is made, and the more cerebral aspects of one's work, which go in through the ears, will often take a secondary situation." Besides, as he once quipped many years earlier, "I can't stand the premise of going on in jeans and being real – that's impossible."

There ain't nothing like a Dame: *Cabaret* photocall at London's Palace Theatre, 1968.

Doing 'Time' at London's Marquee Club, 1973: "What I said went. I was young, I was going to burn the world up."

Super-heavy silver V-neck body suit with solid glass-bead fringing, Earl's Court, 1973.

A spot of Japanese mime for the 'Miracle Goodnight' video, Los Angeles, 1993. "I refuse to be thought of as mediocre. That's why the idea of performance-as-spectacle is so important to me."

In 1987, on the back of a poor album, *Never Let Me Down*, Bowie assembled his most extravagant stage set ever, sported a fashionable mullet hairstyle, set off by a more informal suit and suede winklepicker boots, and performed in the shadow of a 40-foot 'Glass' Spider. As in '83, the tour was a huge moneyspinner with crowds flocking to pay homage to top-tier rock royalty, but Bowie was in danger of being eclipsed by his props. Worse still, his quick-change strategies had grown unflattering and cliched. At least a young pretender like Madonna had youth and the element of surprise on her side. "I succumbed, tried to make things more accessible, took away the very strength of what I do," he now says. "I started to appeal to people who bought Phil Collins albums."

Waiting in the wings. Doing 'Time' for another stretch at Wembley Stadium, London, 1987.

Any sense of Bowie's cutting-edge appeal, trumped up during the punk days, had been wilfully abandoned. He became a model of sun-kissed family entertainment, took holidays in hot places instead of being holed up in the gay bars of Berlin, and joined celebrity squares like Mick Jagger and Tina Turner for nights on the town and the occasional collaboration.

Bowie was beginning to bear an uncanny resemblance to Tommy Steele, both in look and attitude, and seemed happy to spend more time in front of the film camera than worrying about music. There were no Angry Young Men in rock anymore, and therefore no edgy competition for Bowie to spar with. The air of revivalism had even rehabilitated The Beatles, who'd been virtually ignored during the previous decade.

Ms Ciccone inducts David into the Rock & Roll Hall Of Fame, 1996. "It's not just the mass marketers who make fashion, it's the stars: Bowie and Madonna are geniuses at this. They are the ones who make us all try harder." - streetwear designer Tommy Hilfiger.

Facing page: One of Bowie's Glass Spider scarlet linen suits, lined in black chiffon, was auctioned with matching collarless silk shirt at Christie's of South Kensington for £1,800 in 1998.

Following pages: The way you wear your hat. A Sinatra-esque Fifties look for 1986's 'Absolute Beginners' video. "You're never alone with a Strand," shouted an assistant, referring to the cigarette ad. Bowie misheard it as "You're never alone with a band" and promptly formed Tin Machine. *Tin Machine* (1989): Baal in a designer suit, basically.

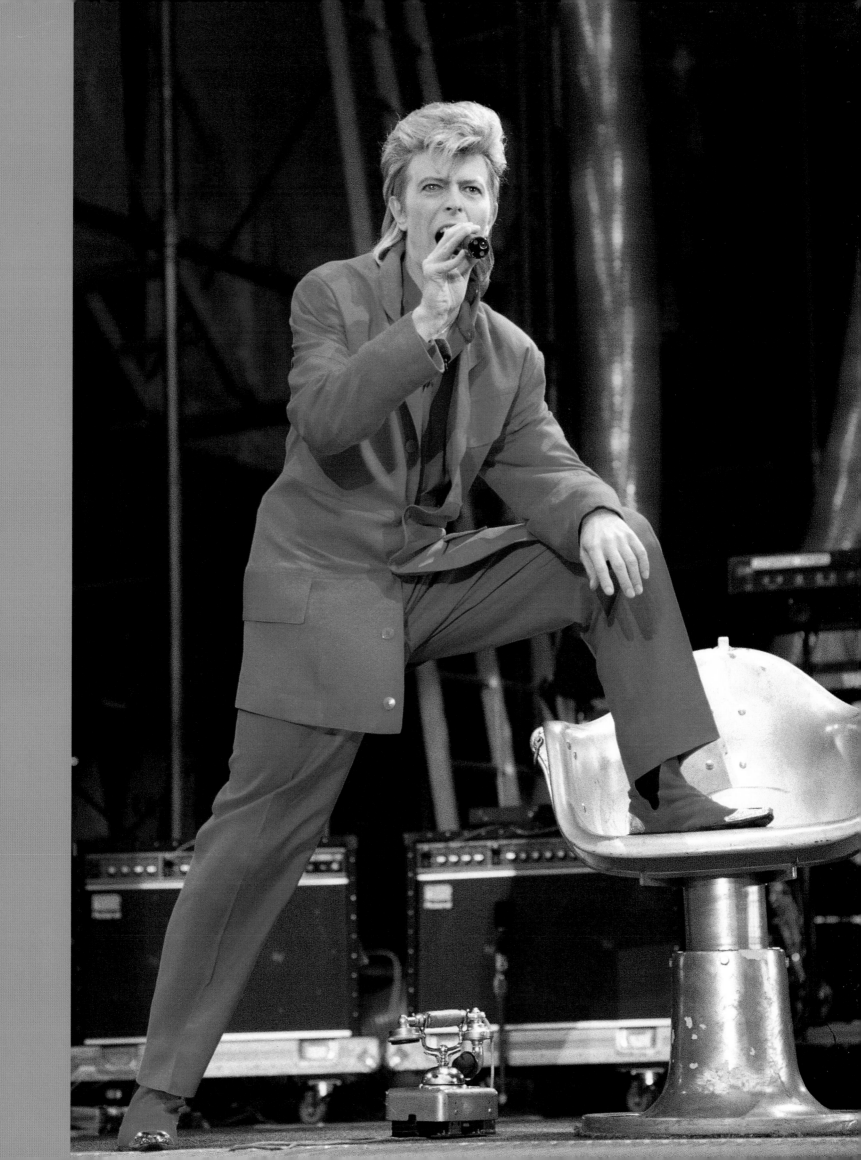

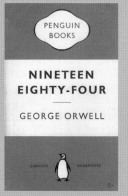

THE BOOKS I READ

Bowie, who has lately described himself as "a born librarian with a sex drive", was first encouraged to read by his father, who introduced him to classics of Western literature such as Thackeray, Shaw and, so he says, French writers like Voltaire and Rousseau. Bowie soon discovered that he preferred less formal, "stream-of-consciousness" writing because, he said, it allowed more room for interpretation. By 1976, the man The Times dubbed "T.S. Eliot with a R&R beat", had a personal library of some 5,000 books. Today, his enthusiasm for literature hasn't waned a bit, and one of his most recent internet wheezes has been to review books online.

Robert Heinlein
Bowie became fascinated with Robert L. Heinlein's *Stranger In A Strange Land* during his months spent touring *Aladdin Sane*. He described the book's central character, Michael Valentine Smith, as "a peace and love messenger from another planet", and claimed he was about to land the role in a forthcoming film. In fact Smith was a power-fixated alien whose fantasies of creating a religious movement end when he is beaten to death by an angry crowd. Any film idea was, in the book's argot, quickly "discorporated".

"He knows everything. He's so well read it's ridiculous. You just sit there and you feel quite a worm in comparison." - Suede's Brett Anderson.

William Burroughs
One of the most memorable scenes in the 1975 BBC TV documentary *Cracked Actor* is when Bowie demonstrated how he wrote his lyrics using the "cut-up" method. It wasn't his invention; painter-writer Brion Gysin is generally credited with the idea. By randomly juxtaposing words and phrases from various sources, cut-up enthusiasts sought to unlock deep truths that lay beneath the ordered text. It leading advocate was William Burroughs, the Beat Generation guru hellbent on destroying all rational thought.

Bowie, who would read out passages from Burroughs' *The Wild Boys* during the *Diamond Dogs* sessions, struck up a friendship with the writer after *Rolling Stone* magazine fixed up a meeting between the two (photographed by Terry O' Neill, and which Bowie, taking on Burroughs' look, re-created nearly twenty years later with Brett Anderson for *NME*) later published as "Beat Godfather Meets Glitter Mainman". "*Nova Express* really reminded me of Ziggy Stardust," Bowie told the author, who probably had a right to look puzzled. But the musician's enthusiasm was genuine: "I derived so much satisfaction from the way he would scramble life," he said after Burroughs' death in 1997. Bowie returned to the cut-up method for much of his Nineties work, though he now uses a computer programme rather than the scissors-and-paste approach.

Christopher Isherwood
Isherwood's *Goodbye To Berlin* provided much of the source material for Cabaret, the 1972 film that revealed parallels between Glam's campy artifice and the showy decadence of pre-war Germany. Bowie's move to Berlin in September 1976 is often ascribed to the influence of Isherwood's writings.

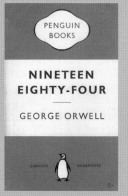

George Orwell
1984 – The Musical? That was going to be Bowie's first major post-Ziggy project until George Orwell's widow refused to play ball. His interest didn't go to waste, though. The influence of the classic anti-totalitarian novel was noticeable throughout much of *Diamond Dogs* (most obviously on '1984' and 'Big Brother'), and inspired both the *1980 Floor Show*, filmed at the Marquee Club in October 1973, and Bowie's extravagant tour of the States the following summer.

Oscar Wilde

Bowie encountered Oscar Wilde's works on his first visit to Ken Pitt's flat in 1967. Two quotes from *A Picture Of Dorian Gray* (1891) seem particularly appropriate to Bowie's work: "To be the spectator of one's own life is to escape the suffering of life," and "Insincerity is merely a method by which we can multiply our personalities." (Though today he'll probably derive more satisfaction from this fragment of Wildean wisdom: "Every great man nowadays has his disciples, and it is always Judas who writes the biography.")

Jean Genet

Genet's *A Thief's Journal* (1949) was a lowlife classic that blurred the boundaries between crime and art. Bowie's 1972 single, 'The Jean Genie', was a thinly disguised tribute to the Sartre-endorsed writer who was both a convicted felon and openly gay.

Bertolt Brecht

Bowie has played the lead role in Brecht's *Baal* for BBC-TV, recorded an extraordinary version of Brecht & Weill's 'Alabama Song', and once discussed making a film version of *The Threepenny Opera* (1928) with Fassbinder. But most important of all was Brecht's notion of epic theatre, which rested on a belief that – via a string of devices such as directly addressing audiences and frequent musical interruptions – theatregoers should never forget that what they were watching was spectacle. Bowie's music-with-theatre spectacles often had the same alienating effect.

Hanif Kureishi

Born near Beckenham, Kureishi (*right*) had another reason to feel like an outsider in his suburban environment: his parents came from Pakistan. But the inspiration for his debut novel, *The Buddha Of Suburbia* (1990), came from his own generation, the so-called Bromley Contingent, a flamboyant crowd of Bowie and *Cabaret*-inspired decadents who followed The Sex Pistols. When the BBC commissioned a four-part series based on the novel, Bowie jumped at the chance to write the music, eventually releasing an acclaimed album on the back of the broadcasts, in late 1993.

Jack Kerouac

On The Road (1957) was the first stop on any young radical's road to freedom during the Sixties. Women, dope, hipster talk, a life of constant change and a search for who knows what – that was eternal, the themes engaged the teenage David Jones, given the book by his half-brother Terry.

Bowie as Baal,
August 1981.

The LA launch concert for 1991's *Tin Machine II* LP. "I never really thought I was cool. I always thought I was vulgar, with a veneer of class."

Facing page: Despite what this picture may suggest, Bowie does read fan magazines.

Soundchecking at the Freddie Mercury Concert For Aids Awareness, Wembley Stadium, April 1992.

"You can't go on stage and live - it's false all the way. I can't stand the premise of going out in jeans and a guitar and looking as real as you can in front of 18,000 people. I mean, it's not normal!"

3.2

Futures & Pasts

Out of sight during the Sixties, out of sorts during the Seventies and out of character during the Eighties: as the Nineties began, David Bowie came dangerously close to becoming out of fashion. His latest project, a designer rock band Tin Machine, of which Bowie was, he maintained, merely one fourth part, had been conceived in a bid to erase the showbiz years and regain an edge to his appeal. Unfortunately, while his new partnership with guitarist Reeves Gabrels showed some potential, the project failed amid poor sales and heaps of critical abuse.

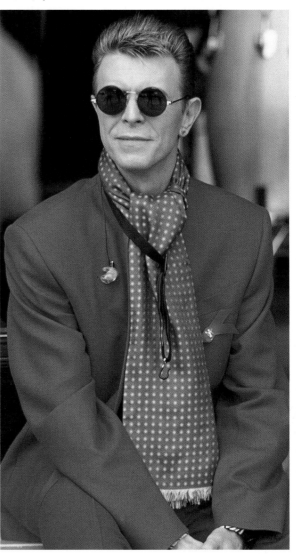

"He had this T-shirt on that said 'Fuck You I'm In Tin Machine'. I wanted to go up to him and point to the shirt and say, Yes, but does anyone really care?" - comedian Vic Reeves.

Join The Gang. Tin Machine's final photo session, by Sukita, February 1992. Bowie, in Thierry Mugler suit and Jean-Paul Gaultier spectacles, would later reflect: "They charged me up. Then personal problems within the band became the reason for its demise. It became physically impossible for us to carry on."

In some ways, the cynicism with which Tin Machine was received set the tone for the decade. Bowie's stylistic changes back in the Seventies may not always have pleased the cognoscenti all the time, but that work was usually received in a context of inquisitive artfulness. Critics found it difficult to be quite so generous to his Eighties work, claiming it rang of cash-registers and creative emptiness. Bowie's activities have been plagued by suspicion ever since. What might once have been acclaimed as a strategic masterstroke is as likely now to be regarded as the latest twist in the desperate plot to keep Bowie visible and credible.

Following pages: On stage in the Nineties. Tin Machine's It's My Life tour at Brixton, November 1991. The one-time King Bee in Hermes shirt, Mugler jacket and bespoke striped luminous Levis.

The Outside tour at Pittsburgh, September 1995. In his 'Painter Man' overalls, tastily topped off with mock snakeskin plastic jacket, originally designed for the 1978 tour by Natasha Kornilof.

Mandarin style at the Rock Torhout festival, Belgium, July 1997.

The Nineties has seen the emergence of a quite different Bowie, one who, after years of pillaging guises and styles from others, has derived his raw material from his own career. In synthesising his cultural trailblazing of the Seventies and the clean-up boy of the Eighties, he's struck perhaps his most uncharacteristic pose yet: a David Bowie who finally seems at peace with himself. This seemingly unholy union has brought with it some dodgy, George Michael-styled facial hair and a good deal of tiresome, publicity-seeking internet activities, but all this seems churlish when measured against the balancing act he's seemingly achieved between private contentment and worthwhile public works - not to mention occasional flashes of revived musical genius.

Therein lies a degree of truth, and one that may apply equally to contemporaries like Mick Jagger, Neil Young and Lou Reed. Yet because none of these ever made the issue of stardom an integral part of their artistic mission, their longevity tends to be regarded with a transparency that is rarely extended to Bowie, who is regarded as arch and studiously gifted in the art of self-preservation. Unfair, yes, but kind of understandable.

During the early Seventies, Bowie gave the guise of being controlled and manipulative when in fact he flailed about in a vortex of fame and infamy that threatened to destroy him. His audience recognised the cracks and celebrated him for living a knife-edge existence where his 'self' was in a state of perpetual collapse. Everything he'd invested in his Ziggy and Aladdin creations - apocalyptic fame, divided self, death-drive - rebounded back on the all-too human David Bowie, who spent the rest of the decade attempting to make sense of his lot.

"The union jacket was designed by myself and Alexander McQueen. I wanted to recontextualise Pete Townshend's jacket of the Sixties, but then I got a bit carried away and thought it would look rather nice as a frock coat. Then Alex got even further carried away and cut bits of it up. I thank you."

In 1996, Bowie's hair made an atavistic journey back to the flame orange upswept brush cut of the Ziggy years. The dandy frock coat, lined with black velvet, was another McQueen creation.

Tired Of My Life. "I'd hate to be like Bowie, singing 'Rebel Rebel' at 50, looking bored." - Pete Burns of Dead Or Alive.

Photographed by Iman, backstage on the Outside tour in New Jersey, 1995.

In 1994, Bowie ditched the legendary crooked fangs for divine straight-capped symmetry.

The man who once interrupted interviews by worrying about the UFOs outside the window, or dreaming he was destined for dictatorial greatness, is now probably the most avuncular, obliging 50-something in rock. This is a sure sign of a personal exorcism, but it's also a characteristically Bowie-like reflection of the zeitgeist. The detached, untouchable celebrities of old (Bowie, Pink Floyd, Led Zeppelin) seemed largely out of place in the Nineties, when the stars of grunge, Britpop and dance music were notable for their ordinariness. Even Bowie's patronage of younger artists (usually those cut from his distinctive cloth), like Suede and Placebo struck a parental, rather than competitive note.

The last of the Mohicans. A funny smile with some Black Hole Kids in California, 1997.

Rakish Georgian sleeves backstage on the Sound + Vision tour, 1990.

Another change has chimed even more successfully with contemporary trends. Bowie has always been a good talker, but during the Eighties, the subject of his past was virtually a no-go area. As luck would have it, this period of denial ended just as the CD-inspired boom in reissues promised to give a new lease of life to the old guard. When in 1990, Rykodisc, a specialist American label, reactivated 16 of Bowie's previous albums, together with an extravagantly packaged three-CD box set, he came up with the perfect marketing strategy: he set off on a six-month world tour to promote the catalogue, offered his audience a chance to vote for the songs he should play, and insisted that he'd never perform them ever again. Inevitably, that promise was broken, but in reminding the world of his substantial body of work, much of which had travelled well (though not 'The Laughing Gnome', which *NME* tried desperately to get included on his set-list), Bowie managed to banish some of the stale odours that lingered from the Eighties.

Facing page: Dipping his gaily painted toes into outré androgyny once more. Backstage at the Phoenix rock festival, July 1997.

Following pages: David in theatrical black, on stage at the Manhatten Center Ballroom where he played a brief set in September 1995 during a benefit show to celebrate the anniversary of Joseph Papp's Public Theater in New York.

Fashionably unshaven, Bowie played Bernie in the stylish Manchester gangland flick, *Everybody Loves Sunshine* in 1998.

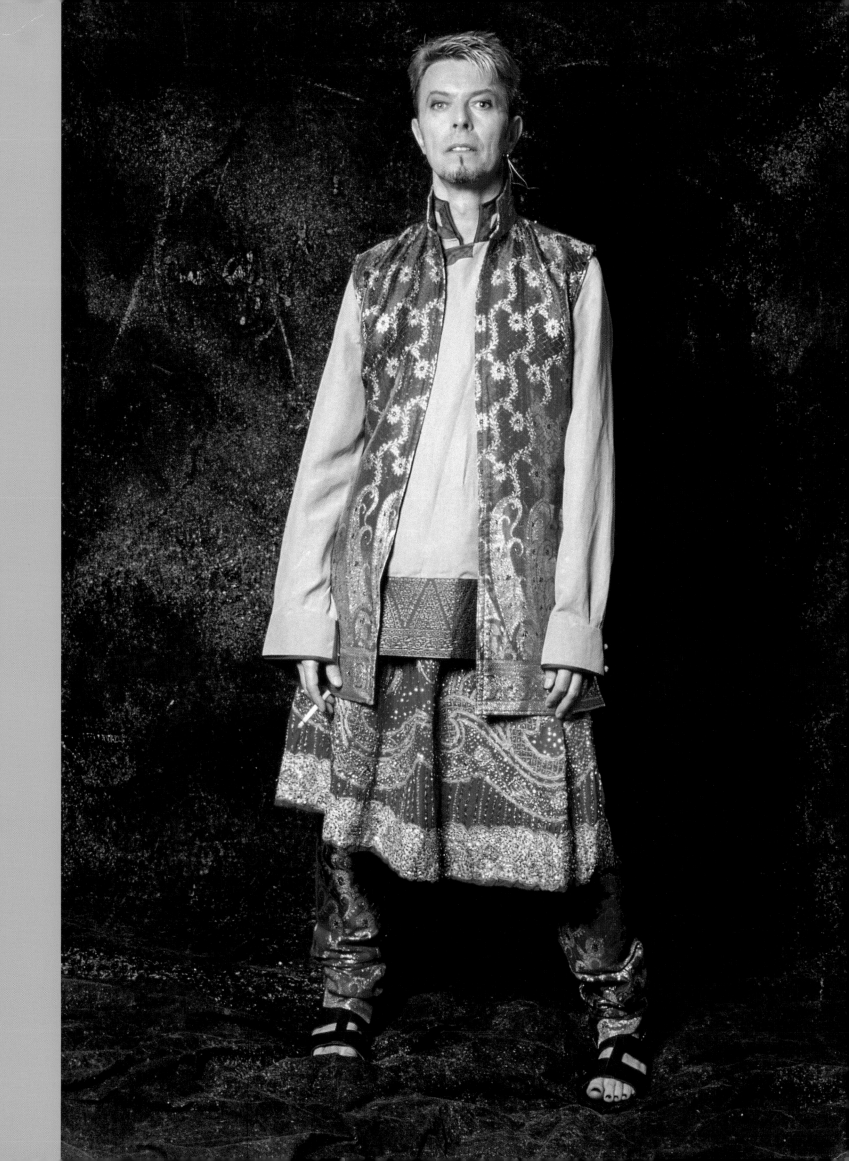

Facing page: I'm Not Losing Sleep. In Neil Young-style lumberjack shirt at New York's Chung King Studios, 1999.

With Jarvis Cocker, London, November 1995.

Left: Bowie received an honorary doctorate at Boston's Berklee College Of Music in May 1999.

He has also benefited from rock's own renaissance. Early in the Nineties, Nirvana popularised his 'The Man Who Sold The World', performing a thrilling version of the song on the band's MTV *Unplugged* swansong late in 1993. Back home, Suede invoked the spectre of Glam Rock, and invited Bowie to join the press party. The Industrial/Metal interface, best represented by the punishing drive of Nine Inch Nails, found its way into elements of Bowie's 1995 album, *Outside*, most notably on 'Hallo Spaceboy', probably his most dramatic recording in 20 years. Then, on 1997's *Earthling*, he appropriated the distorted, contorted rhythms of dance contemporaries like drum & bass star Goldie on a handful of cuts. Oddly, while Bowie's cut-and-paste working method has a lengthy pedigree, and the emergence of the DJ as musical creator has depended largely on creative plagiarism, this seemed to bypass most reviewers who claimed that the move was that of a desperate man. That was a pity, for *Earthling* is surely Bowie's most vibrant, surprise-filled album since 1977's *Low*.

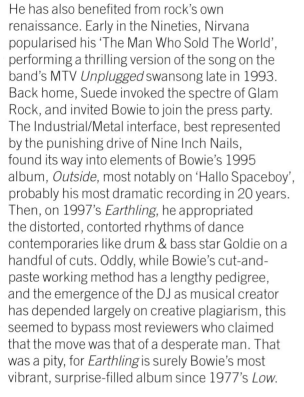

The Nineties also saw an explosion of Bowie's desire to become a cultural all-rounder. He has never been busier. While his albums tend to be biannual affairs, he maintains a regular film career, despite insisting that these endeavours are little more than "a distraction". His profile as an art critic and an exhibiting painter, not to mention his collaborations with BritArt buddies, has gained him a foothold in the art world mainstream. He also has his own Internet Service Provider, which means that thousands of email addresses around the world bear his name (davidbowie.com). He maintains houses in several parts of the world and co-writes songs with fans over the net. He baffles club audiences with sets of new material and is a pillar of music industry respectability. He is an avatar of cultural plunder and a complete one-off. He is David Bowie and he's a particularly precious kind of butterfly.

The male stiletto at The Brit Awards, London, February 1996: "I learned to walk in high heels over 25 years ago. They're Katharine Hamnett's new line. Lovely, aren't they?"

50th birthday VIP party at Julian Schnabel's New York residence, January 9, 1997, with Iman and Kurt Cobain's widow, Courtney Love.

Following page: In October 1999, Bowie received the Commandeur des Arts et des Lettres, France's highest cultural honour. "Some people say Bowie is all surface style and second-hand ideas, but that sounds like a definition of pop to me." - Brian Eno.